# A YEAR
## IN THE
# WOODS

# A YEAR
# IN THE
# WOODS

## Twelve Small
## Journeys Into
## Nature

TORBJØRN EKELUND

TRANSLATED BY BECKY L. CROOK

**GREYSTONE BOOKS**
Vancouver/Berkeley/London

First published in English by Greystone Books in 2021

First paperback edition printed in 2023

Originally published in Norwegian as *Året i skogen—
En mikroekspedisjon*, copyright © 2014 by Cappelen Damm

English translation copyright © 2021 by Becky L. Crook

23 24 25 26 27    6 5 4 3 2

Greystone Books Ltd.
greystonebooks.com

Cataloguing data available from Library and Archives Canada
ISBN 978-1-77840-076-6 (pbk.)
ISBN 978-1-77164-512-6 (cloth)
ISBN 978-1-77164-513-3 (epub)

Copy editing by Lucy Kenward
Proofreading by Stefania Alexandru
Cover and text design by Belle Wuthrich
Cover images by Noli Molly and Kate K. / Adobe Stock

Printed and bound in Canada on FSC® certified paper at Friesens. The FSC® label
means that materials used for the product have been responsibly sourced.

Greystone Books thanks the Canada Council for the Arts, the British Columbia
Arts Council, the Province of British Columbia through the Book Publishing Tax
Credit, and the Government of Canada for supporting our publishing activities.

This translation has been published with the financial support of NORLA.

Greystone Books gratefully acknowledges the xʷməθkʷəy̓əm (Musqueam),
Sḵwx̱wú7mesh (Squamish), and səlilwətaɬ (Tsleil-Waututh) peoples on
whose land our Vancouver head office is located.

"There was no particular line of thought in my mind, nor did I expect to carry out any certain activity or to see anything special along the way. There were no appointments, no plans, no one else who was going to join me. Every decision was up to me alone to make."

**TORBJØRN EKELUND**

# CONTENTS

A walk in the woods  2

**PART I: WINTER**

**January:** The sound of silence  16
**February:** The light returns  28
**March:** The dream of the wilderness  50

**PART II: SPRING**

**April:** The not-so-quiet of the woods  72
**May:** Civilization and its discontents  88
**June:** Nature's secrets  107

**PART III: SUMMER**

**July:** A life out of doors  136
**August:** Legacy  157
**September:** Camp life  173

**PART IV: FALL**

**October:** A theory of two seasons  196
**November:** The last man on earth  209
**December:** The end and the beginning  223

**Appendix:** An office worker's wilderness tips  238
Notes  247
Sources  249
Gratitude  255

Nature: the portion of existing reality that was not cultivated by humankind, but which originated and developed organically; the opposite of culture.

**THE GREAT NORWEGIAN ENCYCLOPEDIA**

*(STORE NORSKE LEKSIKON)*

# A WALK IN
# THE WOODS

WE REFER TO grand wilderness undertakings as expeditions. It seems that more and more people are setting off on expeditions nowadays. But those who went on expeditions in the early 1900s often reported that things used to be different. Back then, explorers went alone. Mere mention of their plans was enough to make the headlines. An entire nation's citizens would follow the explorers from their sofas, enraptured, and when they returned—if they returned—they were worshipped as demigods. Modern explorers by contrast are rarely if ever given an interview and instead have to write an extensive travel blog that competes for readership with hundreds of other blogs.

Still, the word "expedition" carries with it a ring of something grand and important, even today. It has associations in our minds with the word "mission." And yet at the same time it embodies a sense of altruism, the feeling that this undertaking is being done on behalf of others, for a good cause, to the betterment of humankind.

Charles Darwin set off on expeditions in the name of science. Roald Amundsen went to see places no one else had ever seen. They returned with useful knowledge. But today, almost every spot on the globe has been discovered and probed. The earth has been mapped down to the last tiny inch, and only rarely do modern expeditions have a purpose other than simply to generate a feeling of personal satisfaction among their participants.

Expeditions must always have a purpose. That's the primary characteristic of an expedition, almost its definition: that it is carried out by people who know where they are going. Starting at point A, they proceed to point B. Between A and B, they will perhaps encounter an unknown number of challenges. Hunger and cold, ferocious beasts, uncontrollable forces of nature. They should preferably carry their own supplies, on a sled or in a backpack. Time is also an important factor. If the expedition never reaches its predefined goal, it has of course failed. And even if the expedition does reach its goal but takes longer than predicted, it is also considered somewhat of a failure.

The Aboriginal Australians operate under a different concept that is diametrically opposed to that of an expedition. The term "walkabout" is not the aboriginal word, but the idea basically describes a walk through the bush or outback without any predetermined goal, with both an undefined duration and route. It might best be described as "ambling about in the wild." Without any intention of time or space, a walkabout is thus the antithesis of a western expedition. This idea appeals to me very much.

When I was little, I spent most of my time outdoors. The way I remember it, nature permeated almost everything I did. It was present in even the tiniest things. In the mosquito bites that kept me awake through endless summer nights. In the intense smell of decay and the rot of wet autumn days. In the mute astonishment when my tongue stuck to frozen metal in the winter, and the shock when I realized I could not pull it loose. I was *in* nature, in a manner perhaps only children are able to be.

Years passed. I dreamt of becoming a famous explorer—the strong, silent type—the first person to set foot on some blank spot of the map. I continued to seek out experiences in the wild. I went fishing. I slept in tents. I went on boat trips and hiked in the mountains. I did all of this, and when I got older, I did even more. I visited deserts and rain forests and volcanoes and lagoons. My eyes saw mountain massifs so enormous that they took my breath away. And yet, none of these experiences left the kind of impression that nature had in my childhood. They didn't sink in and root into my being in the same way. The reason, I discovered, was that a distance of sorts now existed between me and nature. Here I stood, on the outside as an observer, regarding the ice-capped mountains and the steaming rain forests. I was a guest in the landscape. The landscape and I were not inter-twined as we had been when I was a child.

Back then, I never ventured very far. But every day was nonetheless some new adventure. I roamed about in the wilderness I felt belonged to me: a Norwegian lowland forest made up of spruce and deciduous trees, logging roads, small birds among leafy branches, pine trees higher up, swamps and ponds, blackbirds in the spring, mosquitoes in the mild summer evenings, and trout that always seemed to be jumping. I now missed the feeling of being *in* nature because it had meant so much to me early in life. I took it as a sign that all of my strongest memories have to do with nature.

Now I am an adult. I have long since gotten used to spending very little time in the woods, much less than when I was younger. There are long stretches when I don't even think about it at all because there are other, more pressing matters on my mind. My work. But also all of the pickings-up and droppings-off, the birthdays and conferences, over-the-hill celebrations and volunteering, things to be maintained and plans to be made, accounts to be balanced and friends to be invited over for supper. I am a freelance writer. I've spent the past seven to eight years working from my home office on parental leave. In what has been a blissful mix of work and home life, I have ping-ponged around the kitchen like a great, fertile goddess, having a conversation on the phone while cooking oatmeal and holding a child on my hip.

It has been a wonderful life. I have enjoyed it and it has suited me well. But I came to realize that something was missing. The woods had become a place associated with my past.

Our world is comprised roughly of two different components: the human-made and the non-human-made. Culture and nature. That which has originated through technology, industry, and other intellectual endeavors on the one hand. And on the other hand, that which is organic, has come to exist on its own, and which develops and maintains itself without intervention from humankind. If you are like me, whenever you find yourself in one of these parts of creation, you pine for the other.

The idea of nature as a source of harmony and purity is almost as old as civilization. In many ways, such a notion is banal. It is the conceit that our experience of quietude in the woods signals a divide between ourselves and nature, and that nature is something other than us and not something in which we are daily participants. So-called "primitive peoples" hardly thought about it in this way.

The foremost aim of culture is to produce corporeal and mental comfort for those who have created it. It should provide us with access to food and warmth, but also to safety, entertainment, and intellectual stimulation.

That's what culture is: an apartment, a fitness studio, a cinema, a library, a coffee shop, a restaurant, a pub—most of us are surrounded by culture most of the time. Still, we often find ourselves gravitating toward nature whenever we feel the need to disconnect. One of the reasons is that we associate nature with qualities that are in opposition to those of culture:

Where culture generates stress, nature offers rest.

Where culture produces narrowmindedness, nature offers a bird's-eye perspective.

Where culture makes people feel isolated, nature makes them feel free.

These and many other perceptions that we carry to some degree or other have over time permeated our collective view of nature. We live in a civilization and an era in which a walk in the woods is the recommended antidote for almost any form of suffering. We believe in the curative effect of nature, in its ability to heal, to reset us, and to bring us closer to the beings we originally were or were meant to be.

I'm no exception. For most of my life I've held on to romantic notions about a life of solitude in the woods, no matter that most of my experiences thus far have indicated that such a life is neither as free nor as comfortable as I might like to think. On the contrary, nature can be astonishingly *uncomfortable* and things often happen that seem completely meaningless. And yet, even though empirical evidence points toward the opposite, our romantic ideals have a sticking power. That's how it is for me, and for a lot of people I know. While culture is subjected to endless analyses and critical debates, nature is allowed to enjoy an almost universal litany of praise. We love to attribute a heap of positive qualities to our idea of nature, qualities it's not certain truly belong. Why? What purpose does this serve? And what, exactly, is the nature of nature?

It was summertime when I first started asking myself such questions. My family had gone to spend four weeks at our family cabin, and with each passing day, I enjoyed myself more and more. Life at the cabin was simple and practical. It was a life wherein nature dictated what we did and didn't do. Everything boiled down to the weather and wind direction. The temperature. Fishing conditions. Berries and mushrooms. The vegetables in the patch. The evening mosquitoes, the afternoon wasps. As the summer vacation reached its end, an idea began to germinate in my mind.

What if I simply went to the woods?

What if I took a few days off from work, threw caution to the wind, and turned off my cell phone? What if I were to do this throughout the entire coming year so I could really follow the course of nature through winter, spring, summer, and fall all the way until it was winter again?

What if I finally got serious about my dreams of setting off on an expedition?

It wouldn't have to be grand, this expedition.

Couldn't it also be a little one?

Certainly there was ample opportunity for me to step away from everything for a while. In fact, the opportunity was staring me in the face because I live surrounded by wilderness in every direction. The city of Oslo is surrounded by easy-to-reach forests, especially the Nordmarka forest. And once you've grasped how easy it is to get there, the next step isn't all that difficult. This was the thought that had grabbed hold of me. And now that it had started taking root, I couldn't shake it. It grew like a cloud bank on the horizon and my thoughts would turn more and more frequently to the idea. Before I fell asleep at night. The moment I woke up in the morning.

A year in the woods, I said to myself, twelve nights in the Nordmarka forest. I whispered rather than said it out loud, as if it was something unheard of, or something so risky that merely saying it was dangerous. I didn't mention it to anyone else, mostly out of fear for what they might say. What are you planning to do in the woods? they might ask me. Why? What's the point?

Not everyone is able to venture to the poles or climb to the top of Mount Everest. I have a job. I have children and a partner. I couldn't stay away for a long time, nor did I want to. I decided to tailor my own expedition, to craft a micro-expedition adapted to my level of ambition as well as to the external parameters of my life. I settled on the parameters of one single day during each of the twelve months of the year. On the appointed day each month, I would work until lunchtime and then I would go to the woods. By the start of the next workday, I would be back at the office.

It wasn't much, but it was more than nothing. I hoped it would give me the opportunity to see nature up close and fairly undisturbed. That I would be able to really experience the cold and the warmth and witness the seasonal transitions and shifts of light. We most clearly perceive nature in these transitions, and yet they are also the easiest things to miss because they most often occur in the most miniscule of moments. A puff of mild morning air heralding the spring. The sound of dry leaves rattling to announce the peak of fall. Someone busy with work deadlines or carrying groceries home from the store is probably going to miss these brief moments. To experience them requires stillness and attention as well as an openness to one's surroundings, something that stressed-out people don't often have. At least, not in my experience. I am often a stressed-out person.

When the summer vacation was over and we were back in the city, I announced the idea to my family. I tried to come across as authoritative and determined. I said that over the course of the next year, I was going to spend one day during each of the twelve months alone in the woods, and that they would simply have to accept it. I explained why this format was important to me and laid out how it would work. At first, they seemed astonished and asked what exactly I intended to do out there alone in the woods. I said that I didn't intend to *do* anything; I was just going to mosey around a bit, and I could tell by their looks that this was the reassuring response they had been looking for.

I promised there was nothing more to my plan than a simple desire to spend more time in the woods. "It doesn't have anything to do with all of you," I said. They eventually seemed to accept the idea.

Late summer turned to fall. I began to plan. There wasn't much that needed organizing. It wasn't as if I was training to pull a tire behind me up steep hills or harboring ambitions to make my own freeze-dried backpacking food. The only thing to do was assess my outdoor gear and figure out what to bring and where to go. Late into the evening I pored over my map, weighing the various pros and cons of different locations, casting off one idea and quickly finding another. I knew I couldn't venture very far. I didn't have the time. At first this seemed to put me at a disadvantage, but as the weeks passed, I grew more and more certain that it wouldn't matter much. Far away or close to home, off-trail or within a designated backpacking wilderness. When you're alone in a tent deep in a dark forest on a late night in January, you are going to feel like the only human being on earth whether you're forty-five minutes or three days away from civilization.

This, I discovered, was to be the hypothesis of the expedition. *A year in the woods* would be an expedition in which every single component was small. Experiences, distances, timespan—I decided none of them should feel so big as to be out of reach for either me or anyone else who enjoys going to the woods.

I wrote down the keywords "micro-expedition" and "last person on earth" in my notebook and continued to study the map. At last, I settled on a little glacial pond, a tarn, that is a one-hour walk from the trailhead parking lot. I'd taken detours there before to look out for ripples in the pond when fishing had been bad at other spots.

It is a typical pond in the woods, like the ponds one finds in most mixed forests of the Norwegian lowlands. At one end, it's flanked by a dark spruce forest. At the other, the woods are more open, a blend of long, slim pine trees and birches.

Open moors and swamps. An occasional gleaming hill-crest. The pond I chose is encircled by marshes and peat bogs. Cotton grass grows there in the summer, and in the fall it's possible to find an occasional cloudberry. Bilberry grows a bit deeper in the forest where the ground is harder. There are trout in the pond too, not many, but they are there. Waterlilies bob in the inlets.

The pond was perfect for my micro-expedition. I marked an X on the map and decided I would spend the majority of the twelve nights throughout the year in that spot.

The goal of an explorer is wonderfully concrete. Nearly mathematical. You start at one point and must convey yourself forward to another. The shortest distance between two points is a straight line, and this in principle is all that one needs to follow. I'm not saying an expedition is easy, but the basic plot is no more complicated than a children's book. From this perspective, *a year in the woods* would be a kind of anti-expedition. I planned to visit the same spot several times, a spot that was easy to reach, that lots of people had seen before, and that was not exactly a spectacular location. Whereas an explorer travels in a straight line, I planned to go in circles. And I did not have any noble intentions to brag about. The aim of my expedition was not for the sake of humanity or science; it wasn't even for the good of those closest to me. It was for myself alone. And yet, I was convinced that something would emerge from this expedition that might hold meaning for others too.

I selected the Nordmarka forest just outside of Oslo because it's very close to where I live. It is not the forest of my childhood, but it is very similar. I simply didn't have the time to travel farther away. In addition, the purpose wasn't for me to discover new places. Quite the opposite, in fact. I intended to visit the same places over and over again because I knew that if I paid enough attention, they would have changed slightly each time I went. The forest is a short drive from my house, and that's how it is for most people where I live. It is a privilege, one we rarely consider. The forests are everywhere—big ones and small, thick and more sparse, untouched and cultivated. One has only to venture in.

I viewed these twelve days as a personal nature preserve, a protected region of my life for the coming year, defined not by area but by time. A temporary preserve. I expected the boundaries of my preserve to be under constant siege from the many tasks of culture, but I was determined to defend it.

This was my plan.

Thus, at lunch hour on a Thursday afternoon in the middle of January, I turned off my computer, packed a backpack, and set off on the first stage of the expedition.

# PART I

# WINTER

# JANUARY

## THE SOUND OF SILENCE

"A vast silence reigned over the land. The land itself was a desolation, lifeless, without movement, so lone and cold that the spirit of it was not even that of sadness. (...) It was the masterful and incommunicable wisdom of eternity laughing at the futility of life and the effort of life. It was the Wild, the savage, frozen-hearted Northland Wild."

**JACK LONDON,** *WHITE FANG*

THE SECOND HALF of January. A Thursday, slightly past noon. It was just another average workday, but not for me. There I was, walking along a logging road surrounded by snow-laden spruce trees. The snow was piled three feet deep. The ice was white and gleaming. No one else was around.

The road wound steadily uphill, which is what you should expect if you plan to enter the Nordmarka forest: an upward slog. The best way to deal with it is to consider the ascent an investment in your return.

On my shoulders was a heavy backpack, one of several pieces of outdoor equipment I'd picked up over the fall season. My pack contained a number of items I had thought might come in handy for the day ahead. Some were self-evident; others less so. A sleeping bag, sleeping pad, and tent, of course, but also a large knife, a lot of food, various layers of clothing, a headlamp, cooking stove, book, travel towel, camera, tripod, mittens, toothbrush, seating pad, and a coffeepot.

The backpack was extremely heavy. Every time I took a step, it creaked. On my feet were a pair of winter boots that the seller claimed were the kind used by runners in the famous Iditarod sled dog race through Alaska. The Iditarod boots creaked too. *Tchi-tchi* they said each time they landed on the dry snow.

I had grand expectations for the kind of thoughts I was going to have on these overnight hikes. I was certain they were going to be big thoughts, bigger than the ones I tended to have back home in the confines of my office. Instead, here I was, walking along to the constant creaking of my backpack and boots, unable to produce a single coherent thought. I heard my own breathing and pulse and a type of rhythm that more than anything else reminded me of the carnivalesque street music you sometimes encounter in large cities, the kind where fourteen instruments are being played simultaneously, ten to twelve of them homemade.

I was an orchestra in the woods.

The logging road swung sharply to the left and then flattened out. I paused, leaned back, and let my backpack sink into the tall snowbank. I pulled out my water bottle and rested against my pack. The creaking noise stopped, and everything fell totally silent.

As I drank, my thoughts circled closely to an idea that I would continue to ponder on every one of my hikes in the coming year: the idea of nature as an arena for grand realizations is nothing but pure, romantic fiction. Perhaps our heads don't, in fact, fill up with great thoughts when we are walking alone in the woods. What if it's precisely the opposite? What if our heads are rather *emptied* of any big thoughts and this is what we experience as liberating? If any thoughts do manage to get produced in there, in my experience they are always of the simplest sort. Warm, cold. Light, heavy. Wet, dry. Happy, sad. Hungry, full. Tired, awake.

I sat leaning against my backpack on the snowbank. Over the previous months, I had spent a lot of time thinking about this exact moment and the day ahead of me. I had tried to anticipate what might happen. The cold and the dark. The sensation of being utterly alone in the woods. I've often been in the woods, many times alone. But never in this way, never alone at night in January. Still, I felt well prepared. The fact that I hadn't anticipated the creaking noise of my backpack and boots wasn't something I chided myself for. There are limits to self-discipline and self-awareness, even for someone who is undertaking an expedition.

After a brief struggle, I restowed the water bottle and managed to pull the pack onto my shoulders again. I had been sitting for about ten minutes. When I had sat down, I was soaked through with sweat. Now, of course, I was freezing. I started to walk again and immediately the creaking noises resumed. The orchestra was on the move, the tour continued.

After a while I was warm again and fell into a good rhythm. I felt strong and crazy and slightly ridiculous at the idea of sleeping alone in the middle of the woods in January when there was no need. And also: spending only a single night is hardly impressive. Some people spend months and years alone out in the wild without the urge to tell anyone about it. Nevertheless, I felt satisfied as I walked along the logging road. I pushed my thumbs under the shoulder straps of my pack, lifted my head, and looked around. The sky was partly cloudy, and the day was calm with temperatures of about seventeen degrees Fahrenheit. The snow gleamed between the trees. I took pleasure in the thought that I was in this place in this very moment, in the middle of a work-day. I scoffed at everyone who was in an office at that very moment, forced to wear those tight dress pants that make your thighs feel itchy. I scoffed at what I myself had been only the day before, and what I would return to being tomorrow.

After half an hour, the terrain evened out and the dense woodland opened up. To the north, forested hills rose toward the bright sky. Bordering the west side of the logging road was a frozen body of water. I walked until I reached the northern tip of the lake, where I stopped to eat lunch. I took out four pieces of crispbread and a tube of cheese. In Norway we enjoy *tubeost*, which are essentially soft, creamy cheeses packaged in a toothpaste-like tube. They come in a variety of flavors, such as bacon-cheese, ham-cheese, chicken-cheese, prawn-cheese, bell-pepper-cheese—even super-bacon-cheese, taco-cheese, and burger-cheese. I squeezed a scandalous amount of tubed bacon-cheese onto each slice of bread.

A river joined the lake near where I sat. The mouth of the river was still ice-free, so I walked down and refilled my water bottles there. If this had been summer, the trout would have been rising. But it was not summer; it was mid-winter and freezing cold. My path hadn't crossed with any other human and no other tracks were visible in the snow. The time was just past one o'clock. It would be dark in only a matter of hours.

I was eager to set up camp before the light was gone, so I ate my food quickly and kept walking. The way led me up, up, up. There was always another hill, and I would have liked to leave the logging road, but the snow was three feet high beneath the trees and it was impossible to walk through it without snowshoes or skis.

By three o'clock, I reached the campsite by the pond. I had chosen this site for no other reason than it was a nice spot that few people visited. And it wasn't so far away from the city that I couldn't make it back in time for work the following morning without having to get up at three a.m.

I was sweaty, so I changed out of my damp wool clothes and into a dry set from my backpack. It was impossible to imagine that I might get cold later that night, but it's often like that, in my experience. Whenever I feel well fed, I can't imagine feeling hungry again. That's how the brain works. It is quick to learn certain things. Other things, we never seem to learn.

I put my backpack down on the snow and started to take out the things I'd brought along. Tent, sleeping bag, sleeping pad. Stove and headlamp. An extra change of wool long johns, extra socks, a shell jacket, shell pants. A package of crispbread and the tube of bacon-cheese. Instant mashed potatoes and bacon for dinner. A bag of nuts. A bar of milk chocolate. Coffee. A slug of whiskey, brought along to help me sleep if the dark and unfamiliar sounds caused my nerves to become too active. The tent and sleeping pad were solid and new. It was my sleeping bag that worried me. It was old and well used. The fibers had been squished together after years stored in a compression bag in the shed. The tag told me I should be comfortable down to fourteen degrees Fahrenheit, but I knew it was common practice for manufacturers to exaggerate claims like these. Besides, it was already fourteen degrees out and it was sure to get colder overnight.

As soon as my body heat from the hike subsided, I began to notice the cold. I gathered pine branches to put beneath my tent on the snow. The branches were frozen through and cracked like dry knuckles, so I didn't need to use my knife to break them. I set up the tent without any problems. I couldn't put the stakes in for the guylines, but it was a free-standing tent and so it didn't much matter. I kicked a bit of loose snow over the fabric along the sides and decided that would be enough. It looked professional.

The Norwegian outdoorsman Lars Monsen writes in his book *101 Wilderness Tips* that the first thing you should do when you arrive at a new campsite is light a fire. I realized he had a point, because if anything might be considered remotely comfortable on this January afternoon, it would be a warm fire. I had brought along some wood chips, but no logs. While packing at home, I'd neglected to consider that any dead or fallen branches would be buried under three feet of snow. You can always find dry branches close to the spruce trunks, but these are thin and burn quickly. In addition, mild weather from the previous days had resulted in a thin layer of ice that now coated the branches. The branches had gotten wet and then frozen solid. I warmed some of the thinnest twigs in my hand and put them aside. I warmed a few that were thicker and put them aside too. I placed a few spruce branches onto the snow. I positioned the wood chips from my shed on top of the branches, forming a nice pyramid shape before I lit them. The chips burned as expected, but as soon as I placed the twigs from the spruce trees on top, the flames hissed and fizzled because of the ice.

Every year while I was in elementary school, each of us students was instructed to cut out a round piece of cardboard that we would then section off into four equally large pieces, one piece for every season of the year. Each month would fall into one of these four seasons. After this was done, we then fixed an arrow to the center of the circle, and four times a year our teacher would instruct us to push the arrow around to the next season and the corresponding month. The fact that I still remember this says something, I think, about the number of entertainment options available to us in the 1970s. On my cardboard cutout, January was always slightly to the left of the top, about halfway between the eleven and twelve o'clock positions. It is the first month of the year, named for the Roman god Janus, a derivation of the word *iuana*, which means "door" or "opening," the beginning of something new.

From where I now sat, there was little if anything to signal beginnings. There was no movement, no sign of life. Other than the smoke, there was no scent lingering on the air because everything that has an aroma in nature—leaves and bark and earth and grass—was buried deep beneath several feet of snow. Frozen, packed in ice, solidified.

At three thirty, it began to get dark. It was utterly still in the woods. The only sound was a faint, monotonous whispering noise. Perhaps this was the sound of silence, a whisper from the universe, that basic, underlying keynote of the earth. Perhaps it is always there, this sound. It is so rare that I find myself surrounded by enough silence to really hear it.

Darkness fell quickly. It was as if the light had been yanked out of the landscape, as if it had seeped down and vanished into the soil. All of a sudden it was just gone, and it happened at an astonishing speed. For the few minutes prior, the sun had turned pink, violet, and purple. And then the world became a palette of grays, every shade between black and white. At the same time, I could feel the temperature sinking. All of this in mere seconds. I could feel the change on my face; we say that frost *bites* for a reason. The ice in the pond began to crack. I recall this sound from when I was young and my grandfather would take me ice fishing. It is the sound of ice being formed. Deep booming noises rumbling across the white surface. It reverberated like the thunder of distant artillery.

By five o'clock, the darkness was all-encompassing. It was too cold to stay sitting any longer, so I stood as close as I could to the smoking fire trying to figure out what to do with myself. Back home, I had imagined how nice it would be to whittle a few wooden figurines for my kids during my night in the woods, but this was the kind of idea that you conceive of in the warmth of a living room. Standing next to a hissing fire—freezing—I didn't feel like whittling anything. To hell with wooden figurines and their kind, I thought. It was too cold, and on top of that, I'd forgotten to bring my snow pants. I was only wearing hiking pants which were, I now realized, useless in the cold and snow.

Black clouds passed overhead. A wind started to blow. It blew from the north, which meant it first passed over the pond before it reached me. It tore through the campsite. The cold was paralyzing, but I could hardly change locations now. I would simply have to endure it and learn from my mistake for the next time.

It's easy to imagine what I might have done if something like this had happened five hundred years ago and I didn't have the luxury of simply returning the next day to radiant floor heating and insulated walls. First, I would have had to gather enormous quantities of wood, as much as possible, and then I would have had to find something to eat. To me, the first task seemed easier than the second one, but five hundred years ago I would have had to do both, and quickly. If not, I would have been dead before the morning sun peeked over the treetops. A cross-country skier might have found me later, perhaps, stiff and frozen, like an ice-age mammoth. The people who lived here five hundred years ago didn't layer their clothing with a thin merino wool fabric closest to their skin, microfiber in the middle, and a breathable shell jacket on the outside. The perspectives are terrifying.

By nine o'clock, I was inside my sleeping bag. I had been there for the past two hours, reading a book and otherwise trying to pass the time. I was never able to get the campfire really going, and it was too cold to stay outside. So instead, I huddled in my sleeping bag, waiting for it to get late enough to justify falling asleep. Trude, my partner, sent me a text message reminding me that wolves had recently been spotted in this part of the forest. *Ooooooooohhhh!* she wrote, and: *p.s. there's no shame in turning back.* But there is shame in turning back, so I didn't let myself think such thoughts. But I did think about the wolves for a while. I also thought about what a ruthless place wild nature is. Not so much when the insects are dancing across the pond's surface like gold dust in the evening sunlight. Not when the blackbird is singing its clear, fresh April mornings. But in January, nature is ruthless, and perhaps these are the contrasts that best define it. The difference between night and day, cold and heat, winter and summer are so great that it might be too much for a civilized person.

I tried to savor the fact that I was alone in a tent in a dark, cold forest. There's not much more one can do on a camping trip in January in Norway after darkness has descended six hours before one's usual bedtime. The last thought I had before falling asleep was of how much earlier people must have gone to bed before Thomas Edison invented the light bulb.

All throughout the night I woke up from the cold. It was just as I'd feared. My sleeping bag wasn't warm enough and the freezing temperatures prevented me from sleeping deeply. At three o'clock I was awoken by a scream, a scream which was the only real sound I'd heard all day aside from the babble of the river, my creaking backpack and shoes, and the whisper of the forest. The scream originated from inside the woods on the opposite side of the pond. A heart-wrenching shriek, shrill and high-pitched, piercing the silence of the woods. The noise was accompanied by something that sounded like a struggle of wings. Could it be a bird being taken by a fox? I had no intention of crawling out for a closer look, but I felt certain that nothing screams in the forest at three o'clock at night in January without a good reason.

I woke up again at five. It would be hours until the light returned, but I felt rested enough and awake. I overcame my desire to stay in the sleeping bag and climbed out into the icy morning. I boiled coffee on my Primus stove by the light of my headlamp. Then I packed up my things. I stuffed everything into my backpack without trying to fold it neatly and then I started off homeward.

Throughout the coming year, I would often be struck by the same clear thought: there is a world of difference between nighttime and morning when you are alone in the woods. At night, you are inevitably infused with a heavy sense of melancholy. At least, in my experience. Everything comes across as sad and somewhat meaningless, but upon waking up the next morning, my head feels so light that nothing seems impossible. Here are these contrasts once more. So sharp that they, at times, feel almost too heavy to bear.

The sky overhead was clear and filled with stars; the dark clouds had gone away. No moon, but still light enough that I could walk without my headlamp on. It felt good to move again. The warmth spread through my body and my muscles loosened up. I felt light in both body and mind. The only noise to break the silence was the creaking from my backpack and from my boots on the dry, white snow. If I speed up, I thought, I might even be home in time to make lunch for the kids before they leave for school.

# FEBRUARY

## THE LIGHT RETURNS

"Every year, in the third week of February, there
is a day or, more usually, a run of days, when
one can say for sure that the light is back."

KATHLEEN JAMIE, *SIGHTLINES*

I N MY DREAM of the woods, life is comfortable and free.
I wander in solitude from the moment the sun rises until it
goes down again. I whistle rambling melodies and always
have a piece of straw between my teeth. I quench my thirst
from small, babbling brooks. I rest on warm boulders or
under large green trees if it rains.

And then I continue.

When evening falls—for that is precisely what it does in
my dream, it *falls*—I chance across the perfect camping spot.

A grassy knoll that slopes gently downward toward a small lake. Spruce trees speckle the shore: the occasional birch tree, some pine. There is a natural swimming area and, of course, a tiny stream emptying into the lake nearby to offer clear, cold, fresh water. The weather is mild and still, and there's not a cloud in the sky. Mosquitoes have no place in my dream. I set up my tent and light a campfire. I feel like one of the characters out of a Jack London novel. From such books I have no other memory but of an idyll, even when temperatures are below zero. These are authors who can make freezing weather and a scarcity of food sound appealing, and that is precisely how it is in my dream. Even when conditions are uncomfortable, they appear comfortable in my dream, the way it often is in the movies.

Reality is the opposite. When you're off by yourself in the woods, the reality is that you are more often uncomfortable than comfortable. To claim anything else would be a lie. This is what I experienced in January, and so I had no illusions that February was going to be any different. Still from the comfort of your cozy house, where you feel warm and satiated, it's almost impossible to remember that discomfort even when you've felt it so many times before. Why this is the case I don't really know, but it must have something to do with the way that one's present bodily condition affects how the brain functions. If the body says everything's fine, the brain thinks: Okay, if that's what my body says, there's no point in wasting energy arguing about it.

When I returned from my first night in the woods, I was happy just to be alive. It was with a feeling of pride that I drove up and parked in front of our four-person house. I was exhausted, completely unrested, and yet there was a lightness in my body, a sensation resembling euphoria. It was a Friday morning in late January. An ordinary weekday. As I walked the final steps up the walk in the dawn darkness with my creaking backpack on my shoulders and the Iditarod boots on my feet, I probably should have reminded myself that no one else was on my particular wavelength at that very moment and that what I had been through over the previous twenty-four hours was going to have to remain my own private experience.

It was a little after seven o'clock when I walked through the front door. I knew Trude and the kids would be awake, getting ready for a new day at work, school, and day care. I felt as light as a feather. In my head, my accomplishment was grandiose: the fact of survival doesn't go without saying. Anything might have happened to me out there in the woods; it was an enormous blessing that I had returned, all in one piece.

My family's reactions were not at all what I had expected. Trude and the kids were happy to see me the way they are happy to see me after I've come back from taking out the trash or going grocery shopping. It had only been twenty-four hours since my departure, after all, and I've often been away for that length of time in the past. I jumped right in and started regaling the kids with stories about how cold it had been and how I'd heard a scary noise in the middle of the night. They listened with mild interest. And then they went and sat in front of the TV. Trude said, "Let's talk about this more this evening. They have to leave now." She apologized, but, she reminded me, she is simply not all that interested in the woods.

The house grew quiet. The sky above the rooftops in the east was pink. I switched on the radio and drank coffee while I unpacked my gear. One can easily underestimate the task of unpacking a backpack. It takes longer to unpack than to pack your things. On top of that, there's nothing pleasurable about the chore because there's no longer some alluring destination on the horizon for which you are packing. There's nothing left but a humdrum sense of duty. You know it has to be done, that you have to let your gear dry before putting it away otherwise it will get that distinct moldy smell that so much outdoor gear eventually acquires. And because it's all so expensive—all that gear—the least you can do is take proper care of it.

Back in the woods, I had stuffed everything unceremoniously into the backpack by the light of my headlamp. Now I took it out. The various items were freezing cold and damp; they still contained the night's subzero temperatures in their folds. I draped the tent and sleeping bag over chairs in the middle of the living room to dry. To my dismay, I noticed that I'd brought back half the forest. Pine needles and twigs and small, dirty clumps of ice littered the floor and suddenly the entire room smelled thickly of campfire. Anyone who's been on an overnight camping trip in the woods knows about the morning-after-campfire smell, which is totally different from the night-of-campfire smell. It's no longer pleasing, but a sour, almost bitter odor. In the context of a living room, it is completely out of place.

I cracked open a window. Then I swept up all of the debris and tossed it into the garden. After that, I worked for a few hours in my home office until I grew tired and had to take a nap on the sofa. When I woke up, I lay there for a long time wondering about whether this micro-expedition was good for me or not. The discomfort I'd felt in the woods had been quite intense, and there was hardly anything I could do about the cold. Should I give up while I still have the chance? I wondered. I hadn't told many people about my micro-expedition yet, only my family and a few friends. I could deal with the little bit of embarrassment it would cost me to do an about-face, call it quits, give up. I've given up on several occasions in my life and I knew that my whole screwball idea would be quickly forgotten.

After a few days, I began to dream of the woods again. The dreams were just as romantic and unrealistic as always, as though my experience hadn't left the slightest dent on me.

February came. In the days that followed, the temperatures dipped dramatically. A weather website reported temperatures of minus seven Fahrenheit at the campsite near the little pond. The forecasts promised steady highs. It was now so cold I realized something had to be done about my gear. I couldn't possibly sleep outdoors in such temperatures with my current equipment. It was far too cold. It could even be downright dangerous.

I decided to shop for a new sleeping bag. And a pair of men's snow pants, if there was such a thing that wasn't made for snowboarding. It turns out there is in fact such a thing, but I had to visit a military gear website to get a pair. The snow pants were black and made out of synthetic material. According to the tags, the fabric would remain just as warm even if completely soaked through. And that's another thing about the brain. As soon as I read this information on the tag, I thought: That's good because it's highly probable that I am going to get completely soaked through, so of course I need a pair of pants like this.

Choosing a sleeping bag proved a more difficult task. The selection was enormous and there were so many different criteria. It took days before I was finally able to decide on one. I compared prices and brands and weight. The term "comfort rating" came up over and over again in the descriptions and yet no one bothered to explain what this meant. I assumed it indicated the lowest temperature limit, the threshold just before things take a turn toward the unpleasant, that is, just before the person using the sleeping bag starts to get hypothermia. Or, was this perhaps the temperature at which the user of the sleeping bag would breathe their last breath and die? Since it had been minus seven degrees Fahrenheit at the campsite the last time I'd checked,

I decided that minus seven degrees Fahrenheit should be the lower limit. My search continued, and the advice I was constantly offered was this: buy goose down. It's expensive, but if you buy a sleeping bag made from a cheaper, synthetic fiber, it is going to take up so much space you won't be able to fit anything else in your pack.

And that's how I ended up with my orange down sleeping bag. This model from one of the largest sleeping bag manufacturers has an advertised comfort rating of minus seven degrees Fahrenheit and cost about the same as a moped I had when I was a teenager.

There had been a new moon on the first night of my January expedition, but it was hardly visible. Four days after I'd returned, the moon had grown fuller. I followed it with my eyes over the rooftops in the west while the evening news was on. It hung there, white and shining, the bottom right half lit up, the rest of it dark.

The days passed. Soon it was mid-February. The temperatures dropped. The moon grew and grew. The light began to change dramatically, most notably in the afternoons. At dusk, the sky turned pale blue in the west and then faded gradually darker, while in the east it went from dark blue to black.

It was as if the light itself was absorbing the weight from the snow-laden landscape. The sight caused a sensation to flow through my body, a feeling for which it is hard to find a better word than hope. A general, all-encompassing hope on behalf of myself and others. Nature's most prominent characteristic is change. Everything is always shifting—it is the nature of nature to be in constant motion. This is also true of light, though the changes in light follow a rhythm that is the same from year to year. The fluctuation in light each season is the one predictable element in nature. Everything else, it seems, is permitted to take unexpected turns.

The weather was clear and crisp with little precipitation. Occasionally, a single confused snowflake would drop out of the sky. These flakes were so light and dry that they could scarcely reach the ground under their own weight. After that, the temperatures rose again. The sky grew thick with cloud cover. Snow fell. It turned the world white and muffled every sound.

I was fighting a quiet battle trying to clear my calendar so I could take my second, February hike. Something of cultural importance would always pop up, outcompeting my trip to the woods. Finally, however, I was able to carve out an empty slot in my calendar. And by the time I packed my backpack and ventured into the woods once again, it was a completely different world that met my eyes, even though only a few weeks had passed and the season was still only midwinter.

Because my backpack was lighter now, it creaked noticeably less. My experience in January had made me realize that I had packed like an amateur. I was only gone for a day and one night and yet I'd brought along enough food to feed two adults for a week. And yet, I hadn't packed nearly enough clothing.

Or, more correctly, I'd packed the wrong clothes. It had been so cold that I'd been forced to put on every single item of clothing I'd brought, and still I froze. This time, I'd reversed my ratio. I'd switched out excess food for more clothing, but also better and more appropriate clothing. The result was a lighter pack and a more practical setup in general. Food not only weighs more than clothing, it also takes up more space because it's stored in impractical angular packages, while clothing can be balled up to the size of a fist or shoved down into the backpack between other pieces of gear.

In addition to my new sleeping bag and snow pants, this time I'd brought along a pair of thick wool long johns and woolen socks, a thin wool pullover, a wool sweater to layer over that, and a light jacket made out of so-called PrimaLoft material, which is a compressible insulating synthetic fiber. On the outer layer, I wore a waterproof shell. Just in case, I had brought along a second PrimaLoft jacket, as well as extra socks, long johns, and another wool pullover. That, I thought with satisfaction, should probably do it.

After an hour hiking at a steady pace, I passed my campsite from January. From the lack of footprints, I could see that hardly anyone had been there since my camping trip the month before. My own tracks had been covered with fresh snow as well and the entire area appeared completely untouched.

I felt like the first man on earth. A solitary figure in the midst of an unblemished, snow-covered landscape. I felt both privileged and guilty for putting my marks on the scene. Great big boot prints marring the lovely white snow. A bulldozer in the midst of all that beauty. It was still early afternoon. The weather was fair, and now I could also feel the sun's warmth. I was in no particular hurry, so I decided to continue up the trail and then circle back when it started to get dark.

I walked along the kinds of logging roads that crisscross this forest and so many other forests that are close to civilization. I passed huge piles of newly felled spruce trees and breathed in the intense aroma of resin and bark and green needles. Winter is logging season. That's the way it's always been in Norway because the snow creates an ideal surface on which to pull out the heavy trunks. At least this was true when the only means of getting the job done was to use an old horse. Nowadays of course, trees are chopped down by forestry machines that probably aren't limited by the seasons to do what they were made to do. Outfitted with computer programs worthy of a spaceship, they remind me of my son's Transformers toys. Nevertheless, it appears that winter is still the preferred season for logging in Norway. Perhaps it's nothing but old habit lingering over the industry.

The trees that had escaped the transformer-machines were decked with snow, each branch rimmed with a thin line of white. The sky was an even white plain. Although there were no clouds, there was a thin layer of fog. Maybe it had to do with a combination of humidity and cold, I don't know, but something told me the fog was going to break up eventually and so it did. After walking for an hour, I had climbed high enough to be above the fog line. From up there, the sky was a brilliant blue. Here and there, the crowns of trees poked up through the fog, reminding me of the low roots poking out of the snow that you have to watch out for when you go cross-country skiing at the end of winter. To the west, the sky was brighter, almost yellow.

I snapped a few photos and kept hiking. I sensed the lightness I had felt in January, the feeling that my head was gradually being emptied of thought and that my body was becoming the only thing that mattered. The sun beamed down its warmth. The snow melted. I watched spruce branches lift back up to their original positions when the burden they had been carrying suddenly dropped away. I heard the thud when the clumps of snow landed in the deep snowbanks beneath the trees.

This also was a day like any other. There were no other people around, but the silence from January had yielded to bird-twitter. There weren't all that many birds to speak of, of course. One couldn't talk about, say, choirs of birds, and I would be lying if I claimed that my hike was accompanied by birdsong on this February afternoon. There had been birds outside our home throughout the long winter, and for good reason. They tend to come into the more populated urban centers when the woods are buried in snow. They hadn't been very noisy around the house in December and January, but starting in February I often woke to the sound of chickadees singing before dawn.

Some small birds stay in the forests throughout winter, however, and a few of them decided to sing. These individual melodies created a soundtrack that had been absent in the woods in January. I recognized the characteristic tones of the chickadees, but I couldn't identify the others. They sang, these tiny birds, even if there was scarcely anything to sing for. It was still extremely cold outside and there was more snow now than there had been in January. There was a long time yet until the spring, at least it would be long for creatures who perch on tree branches with nothing else to do but whistle.

I walked until I felt hungry. The snow was still three feet deep and packed hard enough to bear my weight only in a couple of south-facing dips. I arrived at a larger lake down in a hollow. The surface of the water was frozen, and a pair of ski tracks sliced across it like dark blue lines across a large white sheet of paper. I saw a solitary skier moving on the opposite side. I think it was a man, and he was cross-country skiing the way people used to in the old days, without the swaying movement that characterizes modern Nordic skiing. Instead, he plopped one foot down in front of the other with his knees stiff, slowly and systematically. He moved the way elderly people do when they are pushing their walkers in front of them across the shiny linoleum floor of a retirement home. Slowly, but steadily. I followed him with my eyes as I ate my lunch. Two quarts of water. Crispbread with tubed bacon-cheese. And for dessert: nuts.

At three o'clock, I picked up my backpack and began the trek back to my campsite. I couldn't imagine staying the night anywhere other than at my original campsite from January. I had spent one night next to the ice-covered pond and by now I felt somewhat at home there. It was a known point in the midst of the unknown and I am the kind of person who always prefers the familiar to the unfamiliar. Sometimes this is a good thing. At other times, it's a disadvantage, not to mention the detrimental impact such a tendency can have on the natural surroundings.

My grandmother has always lived in the woods. Her home is situated next to a large lake in eastern Norway. From her house, it's ten miles to the nearest grocery store. There are only a few other houses nearby and many of these are no longer occupied. My grandmother is surrounded by wild nature and has no other thought than that this is how things have always been. She could never imagine living in a city. Ever since I was a child, she has always said about February: "This is the time when you really have to pay attention; this is the *real* spring, when everything happens." I never quite understood what she meant, since the scene outside my window in February is always a cold, snowy landscape with no hint of letting up. But I've come to believe that what she means is that all the changes leading to springtime first start to become apparent in February. The 21st of December is the darkest day of the year: that's when the sun turns, we like to believe. The days start to get longer. First slowly, then gradually faster and faster. Winter solstice may be the astronomical turning point, but its effect first becomes visible at some point in February. That's when we may see the earliest signs that the great natural processes are turning in reverse, and that a new season is at hand. The light grows bolder. The temperatures rise. Animals and birds slowly come to life again. These, and a thousand other things both big and small, suddenly burst forth and break out in color and in the end manifest in what we like to think of as spring. The anemones that bloom in April are not the spring but rather the result of the spring. I imagine this is what my grandmother meant.

I learned this and many other things from my grandparents when I was young. Back then, I knew more about nature than I do now. I always raised my hand in science class. I was able to name every tree or fish, knew the best time of year for whittling willow flutes, knew which mushrooms were poisonous and which were edible. I could identify the sound of a brown owl and knew how to build and light a campfire. In my class, only one person knew more about the outdoors than I did. Espen often made the headlines of the local newspaper because of things he'd found in the woods or in a ditch or along the shoreline of a lake, and it was always something strange or rare. A stick in the likeness of Olav, who was Norway's king at the time. A carrot shaped like the Eiffel Tower. A fish with an uncanny resemblance to the prime minister. If I remember correctly, it was always some natural object resembling some cultural thing. Maybe Espen had figured out the formula you needed to stir up enough interest from the local newspapers so they would dispatch a photographer.

Personally, I never found anything that qualified as a mention in the local papers. But I did borrow books every time the bookmobile stopped once a week in front of the grocery store near my house. From their inventory, I read Jack London and Mikkjel Fønhus and stories written by other authors whose names I no longer remember. The stories had titles like *The Great Pike in the Reeds* or *The Old Moose in the Deep Forest* or *An Owl Screech in the Valley*. Each book had a rugged but also romantic tone, and they all dealt with topics about humans' relationship with nature and wildlife. Every one of them implied that there was a mysterious connection, that it was possible for these two elements—nature and humankind—to understand one another, and that we could perhaps even become friends if only we took time to be mutually kind and respectful.

I was totally consumed by these stories. They featured fur trappers and indigenous tribes and explorers and dog-sled drivers and gold miners and hunters and fishermen and mountain climbers. I read James Fenimore Cooper's series, some of which were about the war between the British and French in the Great Lakes of Canada in the mid-1700s. *The Last of the Mohicans* is the only one of these five novels that has stood the test of time.

I read Mark Twain's books about Tom Sawyer and Huckleberry Finn, and what all these stories had in common was they were about a character who lived a life in the wild that was free and filled with adventure and altogether different than the life I was living. If I had been perhaps a bit more enterprising, or if I had known someone else who was similarly like-minded, I may have become a famous explorer. But I was not all that enterprising. I was content to read and to dream. I also didn't know anyone else who felt the same rapture in such things that I did. There was only my grandfather, but he came from a generation that rarely, if ever, allowed romantic daydreams to prevail over level-headed, tough-knuckled reality.

I reached my campsite at the pond well before nightfall. Aside from my own prior footprints, four sets of tracks now crisscrossed the site. The tracks originated from the direction of the forest on the south side of the open wetland. They had crossed the wetland, passing directly over the spot where I planned to pitch my tent, before continuing down and across the frozen pond. Three of the sets of tracks were big and deep, not hard to identify because there is only one kind of animal that makes tracks like that in a Norwegian forest: a moose. I bent over and studied the tracks. In the books I read as a child, the Native Americans were able to guess from a single glance at a set of tracks what kind of animal it was. I ran my fingers softly along the edge of the moose tracks. Of course, they were soft because the snow was pure powder. I knew the prints hadn't been there a few hours earlier, so my investigative actions were nothing but pretense. I really had no clue when exactly the animals must have passed by while I was away.

The three sets of moose tracks veered here and there. Each individual animal had quite clearly staggered around, but they also frequently crisscrossed one another's tracks. Two of the sets of tracks were almost equal in size but the third set was much smaller. Perhaps they were two cows and a calf, two bulls and a calf, or a cow and a bull and a calf. These were the only three possibilities, but I decided to stick with the first configuration.

Bull moose are probably not unlike most other males in the natural kingdom, constantly moving on, not spending any more time with the herd than they think necessary for establishing a family. Perhaps these moose had chanced upon each other somewhere in the woods, decided to travel together, and then had crossed my campsite serendipitously, veering this way and that, pausing, walking a bit farther, and then continuing on, the way you see groups of young people milling about and wandering back and forth in groups on the weekends. I assumed they had nibbled some tree buds even though I couldn't see any signs of it. I would like to have seen a moose nibbling tree buds. From a safe distance, obviously.

The fourth set of footprints followed the moose tracks, but in contrast to theirs, it led in an almost straight line. The animal's four paws had left marks in the snow that were nearly identical all the way down to and across the pond. They were much smaller, each pawprint the size of a quarter, maybe a bit bigger. My first thought was a wolf, but I knew the tracks were too small. So it must be a fox, I thought. And it must have passed this way just before or directly after the three moose or, for all I knew, at the same time. If there is a secret connection between moose and foxes, I am the last one to know about it. I said a silent prayer that the little moose cohort would not return this way later that night. Then I turned my attention from the tracks toward my priorities: it was high time to pitch my tent and ready myself for the coming night.

As I set up the tent, the wind began to blow. At first, the sky was totally empty. And then, all at once it seemed, a remarkably strong breeze pushed in. Snow whirled across the lake and sparkled in the last rays of sunlight. The wind was fresh and mild in a sense. It reminded me of many similar experiences I've had at this time of year, especially on days when the weather is beautiful. There was something uplifting about the wind, and in my positive frame of mind, I interpreted it as a sign of spring.

At four o'clock, the wind died down again. I pitched my tent as I had the previous month, securing it with snow and putting down the sleeping pad with my new sleeping bag on top. I was eager to try it out. Made wiser by my previous painful night outside, I had brought along a few birch logs from the shed. In contrast with my experience in January, this time I knew what to expect; it is incredible how little it takes for something to cross from the unfamiliar to the familiar. These states are separated by only a hairline, and there's something to be gleaned from this: a small measure of openness to one's surroundings can quickly render them less threatening.

Once my tent was up and everything prepared for the night, I set about cooking dinner on my camp stove. It was the same fare as the last time. First, on the thigh of my brand-new snow pants, I sliced up an entire package of bacon. Then I fried it in a pot. Once that was done I filled the pot with snow, and after the snow had melted I added more snow until the pot was about half full. I heated the water up with the bacon still in it. When the water began to boil, I turned off the stove and dumped the contents into a packet of instant mashed potatoes. I let the mixture sit for a few minutes, stirred, added salt and a lot of pepper—and then I went to town. It tasted good, even if it got cold before I'd finished eating. For dessert, I had chocolate and while enjoying that, I boiled water for coffee in the same pot that I'd used for the mashed potatoes.

At four o'clock, the sun hovered above the treetops in the west. If this were January, it would already be dark. But the sky was still lit up and I could feel the sun's warmth. Out of nowhere, a fly buzzed past. It seemed out of place amid the white landscape. It landed on my hand and I thought: *a fly!* Soon it continued on its way, toward some unkind fate, I imagined. It had committed a great error, this fly, interpreting the sudden rise in temperature as an invitation to creep out of its hiding spot under a piece of tree bark. Or maybe it just wanted to challenge convention and see whether it could, in fact, survive even though the rest of its species was still hibernating. It buzzed around like a lonely Icarus in the vast, lifeless forest.

The sun went down behind the trees. The temperature dropped, the way it had in January, but this time the light was different. In January, the light had dissipated the instant the sun went down. Now I noticed that the sky remained lit up even after the sun had vanished. I took out the birch logs I'd brought from home and built a fire. They burned so easily, these logs, and the fire got hot enough for me to add more wood that I'd gathered down by the water, which burned even if it was slightly damp.

I sat next to the fire. I felt neither cold nor wet. It could easily have been a scene out of one of those great outdoor books. The sky didn't truly turn dark until after seven, and shortly after that the first stars began to appear. I wanted to wait for the moon, even though I didn't know whether or where it was going to appear. I resolved to learn more about the moon when I returned home. To me, the moon's path across the sky seemed totally arbitrary, changing from day to day. But I knew there must be an order to its movement, and I thought that people like me ought to know how this system works.

I waited until nine for the moon. After that I gave up and went inside my tent. I crept into the new sleeping bag, which was so thick it felt like being encapsulated in a cocoon. I lay reading a book by the American author David Vann. The book was called *Legend of a Suicide* and the text on the back cover stated that the story was semi-autobiographical. A father and a son move to Alaska to live self-sufficiently in a tiny cabin for a year. It's the father's idea. The son is twelve or thirteen years old and doesn't want to go. All he wants is to stay at home and hang with his buddies, like most boys do. But the father is consumed by his idea about how great it's going to be. It never occurs to him to ask his son's opinion; he just assumes that his son shares the same dream. The father is bipolar and suicidal. He's an out-of-touch romantic and not in the least prepared for the inhospitable conditions they face in Alaska. The son is ill prepared too, after all he's just a boy, but he is more realistic than his father.

I read the book for several hours. It was very good. There was a turning point in the story that was so shocking I had to put it down. I won't say more about it. That would ruin it for future readers.

I slept until eleven p.m., full and warm and content, considerably less tense than I had been in January. In the middle of the night, I woke up and had to relieve myself, which often happens to men after they've reached a certain age.

After a lot of fumbling with zippers and Velcro and my headlamp, I was finally able to extract myself from the sleeping bag and climb out of the tent. The woods were perfectly still. There wasn't a single sound; there was nothing but the underlying keynote of the universe, the steady whisper that I'd also heard in January. I stared up at the sky while I did my duty. It was crowded with stars and there, high above the pond, dangled the moon. I gazed at it for a while and then I shuddered, crawled back inside the tent, and back into my new goose down sleeping bag where I slept as happily as a stone.

At one point on my return through the woods the following morning, I heard the distinct sound of chomping from the other side of the high snowbank that ran along the logging road. I crouched down and slowly poked my head up over the pile of snow. Fifty yards away, in a thicket of spruce and naked birch trees, two moose were having breakfast. They had almost certainly heard my creaky boots, but they didn't seem to mind and kept on with their systematic chewing. Both were cows, or maybe one was a cow and one a calf from the previous year. Neither was very large. I lay on my stomach on the bank for a long time, watching. They seemed so clear and harmonious where they stood. A new moose-day was breaking, and the fact that it would in all likelihood resemble every other moose-day didn't seem to bother them. I observed them from behind the snowbank and thought that if moose were airdropped into the landscapes of India, before long they would in all likelihood acquire the same sacred status that cows enjoy in the Hindu faith.

# MARCH

## THE DREAM OF
## THE WILDERNESS

===

"And into the forest I go, to lose
my mind and find my soul."

**JOHN MUIR**

THE DREAM OF leaving civilization in order to live a free, independent life in the wild is possibly as old as civilization itself. People either feel lonely and seek out social fellowship, or else they do the opposite. Where two or three are gathered, at least one of them will eventually start daydreaming about striking out on their own, leaving the others, possibly for good, and setting off in search of a purer life somewhere else. The most well known of such stories is, naturally, the American philosopher and author Henry David Thoreau's book *Walden—Or Life in the Woods*, which was published in the mid-1800s.

Similar books continue to be written today as well, but there are fewer of them. Jon Krakauer's *Into the Wild* is perhaps the most important modern book in this genre. The book became an instant classic. It is a documentary-like narrative of a young middle-class American man, Chris McCandless, who left the relative safety of his childhood home in a suburb close to Washington, DC, to create a new life in the inhospitable wilderness of Alaska. McCandless is only one of many examples of people who consider unadulterated nature as the only true place to be. Their motives might vary, but from recluse to recluse their ideas about what can be gained from such an undertaking are remarkably similar. The basic philosophy, almost without fail, holds that society forces on individuals limitations that do not exist in nature. One must make use of one's body and live in harmony with the elements in order to rediscover something that has gone missing in modern civilization. It's about choosing to live life on the edge in a world where death is never far away.

I've often wondered what has kept me from doing something like that. It's a ridiculous question to ask oneself, embarrassing almost, seeing as I don't have any reason to do anything quite so drastic, and besides, you can be fascinated by someone without needing a reason to imitate their actions. I don't think I behave in a way that signals that society, for its own sake, needs to exile me as quickly as possible. And yet, when I decided in my forty-second year of life to initiate my micro-expedition to the woods, I must admit that my old dream of living life on the edge was still there. The fact that I have never yet realized this dream in a larger format than this micro-expedition boils down to several factors, including that I have possessed a great, almost exaggerated, respect—or caution—for nature ever since I was very young. Even though I was sometimes ashamed of it and tried to shake it off, I was never really able to escape its hold on me.

I wanted to be a daredevil. I wanted to ski fast down unfamiliar slopes, ride in a boat at night without a light or a life vest, fish in new places without a map or enough gear, and wade farther out into the river than was reasonably safe. All the people I knew who did this claimed they were living fuller lives in those moments. It's not unlike BASE jumpers or free climbers who have somehow come to the conclusion that using no protection is the only way to do it. The knowledge that something could go wrong makes the experience more intense. The thought that you might die at any moment gives your life meaning (for the brief period that you are still alive). This is more or less the mindset, and since it's almost exclusively men who think like this, rarely women, there must be some connection here with one's ability to grasp that your life is not only about you. Of course, I have undertaken risky things in my life simply because they were risky. But for the most part, this respect of the unpredictability of nature has stuck with me over the years.

As is often the case, such mindsets are due in part to one's upbringing. And this is why I mention it here, on the third leg of my micro-expedition. Since childhood, I was raised with a mantra that was branded into my being: *Never trust the month of March*. My entire family lived by this saying. I don't know where we got it from or what kind of satisfaction we were meant to glean from it. If we had, in addition, said "Never trust the state" or "Never trust strange men," the statement might have had more context. But it was only ever the month of March we did not trust, the month of the spring equinox and often of Easter, and also the month of the year in which we set our clocks forward one hour so that it, literally overnight, stays lighter until late in the evening. March is the first month of spring.

My father was particularly eager to point out March's notorious unreliability, and there can be little doubt that this need has something to do with his Protestant roots. The future is uncertain; you never know; misfortune may be waiting just around the corner; don't count your chickens; better to be certain first.

Thus, if my family set out on a weekend in March, and if we went to a lake where the gulls hovered like white paper airplanes in the sky and the mild spring breeze caused the tiny weeds clinging to rock fissures to rustle joyously, or if we went to the mountain to cross-country ski atop the last remaining snowdrifts, or if we went to the woods to look for anemones and trudge around in the previous year's dry leaves among south-facing slopes, we would always say: Never trust the month of March. Tomorrow there might be a foot of fresh snow.

Even now, I carry with me this eternal urge to imagine the worst-case scenario. I've tried shaking it off, but it sticks with me, like butter to a slice of bread.

It was high time for the third leg of my expedition. I tinkered around in my home office while keeping tabs on the weather and starting to organize my gear for the next hike. March kicked off with a long-lasting high-pressure system, which in the winter means low temperatures.

Outside it was frigid, and clear. The following days were the same. The ice on the roads in our neighborhood mingled with the dirt and salt and grit and gravel. The snow along the roads was piled three feet high and looked like it would never melt. And it didn't. It wasn't until the end of the month that I finally collected my things and set out for a third night in the woods. I had spent the entire previous day stretched out on the sofa because that's one of those things that can happen when you work from home. There are days when I find myself reading a book or watching a film and I tell myself that this is all a part of my work. It's a privilege I try never to take for granted.

So there I was, stretched out on the sofa with a notebook and a ballpoint pen. First, I watched Werner Herzog's documentary *Grizzly Man*. The film is a compilation of footage taken by the bear enthusiast Timothy Treadwell over thirteen years while trekking alone in Katmai National Park in Alaska. Each summer, Treadwell followed and lived close to a sleuth of bears. He considered himself an honorary member of that sleuth, a friend, a protector of bears. The final footage was taken in September 2003. On October 5th of that year, Treadwell was killed and partially devoured by one of the bears he imagined he was protecting. Herzog narrates the documentary. In the opening scenes, as we see Treadwell and the bears roaming through the magnificent scenery, Herzog says:

> All these majestic creatures were filmed by Timothy Treadwell, who lived among wild grizzlies for thirteen summers. He went to remote areas of the Alaskan peninsula, believing that he was needed to protect these animals and educate the public (...) What Treadwell intended was to show these bears in their natural habitat (...)

> I discovered a film of human ecstasy and darkest inner turmoil. As if there was a desire in him to leave the confinements of his humanness and bond with these bears. Treadwell reached out seeking a primordial encounter. But in doing so, he crossed an invisible borderline.

I watched the film in its entirety and took notes. Here was another doomed adventurer, like McCandless. When the film was over, I found an article that was published in *Outside* magazine in January 1993, the first written account of Chris McCandless's tragic story. The front cover of the magazine was devoted entirely to him:

*EXCLUSIVE REPORT: LOST IN THE WILD*
*On April 28, 24-year-old Chris McCandless walked off into America's Last Frontier, hoping to make sense of his life. Four months later, he was dead. This is his story.*

And the story was told in this article by renowned climber and journalist Jon Krakauer. He had struck a nerve. After it was initially published, the piece garnered so much attention that Krakauer decided to expand it into a book. Three years later, he published *Into the Wild*, which documented McCandless's travels throughout the US, from the time he graduated from college with top grades in every subject and donated his savings to charity before setting off in his old Datsun to when his remains were discovered in a bus in Alaska two years later. In 2007, the story reached Hollywood and was made into a movie. Later, in 2013, in the November phase of my micro-expedition, *Outside* would print a new article about Christopher McCandless, just over twenty years after the first article was published. The title was "The Chris McCandless Obsession Problem" and the piece discussed the pilgrim phenomenon that arose in the aftermath of Krakauer's book. That momentum still has not flagged, and people continue to flock to the old bus where McCandless was found dead. And many of them do it in the same manner as McCandless: unprepared and fatalistically. They are the incarnated inversion of mountain preparedness, these people. Look at us, they seem to say, we refuse to take any precautionary measures; we are so free and unworried that whatever happens, happens; we're just gonna amble along here on the Stampede Trail, off into the wilderness, just like Chris.

At least, that's what I imagine they're thinking. The article in *Outside* reported that many such followers frequently have to be rescued from the wilderness and the old bus because they make the same miscalculation as McCandless: they cross the river when the water level is low, forgetting to consider that it will later rise when the ice-cold floodwaters flow down from the mountains.

Reactions to the fates of both Timothy Treadwell and Chris McCandless are characterized by extreme polarization. Some are adherents to both men's life philosophies (which, ironically enough, ended in both cases with untimely death), and often to a degree that makes them seem almost like disciples. Others are opposed, often to the opposite extreme. Their argument is that McCandless and Treadwell were two irresponsible charlatans who never cared about anyone other than themselves, two egoists who—some claim—got what they deserved. Of course, still others have more nuanced views of the tragic ends met by both men, among these Herzog and Krakauer. As well as the rangers in Alaska, who soberly note that humans cannot befriend bears. And that if you intend to survive in the wild, you first must acquire the necessary equipment and knowledge. Chris McCandless, the rangers assert, had neither.

Jon Krakauer is himself an experienced outdoorsman and climber, and even though he never states it directly, he writes in a way that makes it clear McCandless was brought down by hubris. The basic idea, according to the ancient Greeks who coined the term, was that humans ought to know their place in the cosmos and stay there. If you mess with the gods, or decide to oppose the cosmic order, things may not work out very well for you. McCandless's sister, with whom Chris shared a close and trusted relationship, was the most important source for Krakauer's book. She often repeated that this lack of moderation was a characteristic trait of her brother's, and she suggested she had worried all her life that he was eventually going to do something like what he ended up doing. When Chris McCandless embarked on the Stampede Trail, he broke every basic rule of outdoor survival, the Boy Scout motto "Be prepared," and the most common-sense rules of mountaineering. He did this knowingly and willfully. He brushed off offers of supplies and money to buy food. It's clear that he intended to be unprepared. Maybe he imagined that nature would take care of him.

McCandless was like the fly I had encountered in February. He wanted to challenge the wild and himself, imagining there was some kind of oneness, that it was possible to meld into Nature. Instead, his beloved Nature ended up taking his life. There are obvious parallels with the fate of Timothy Treadwell.

Both men's fates were the result of the arrogance of youth, but also of many years spent reading certain authors and their works. McCandless read the great classics: Charles Dickens, H. G. Wells, Mark Twain, Leo Tolstoy, and Jack London. According to a source in Krakauer's book, one of several people McCandless met on his trip to Alaska, he encouraged everyone he crossed paths with to read London's *Call of the Wild*.

Such is the perspective that permeates the entire story in Krakauer's book but that has vanished in the film. Krakauer is critical of McCandless's hazardous undertaking, but he can still understand it.

My calendar informed me it was Palm Sunday as I embarked on the third phase of my micro-expedition. The sky was cloud-free, cold, and windless. I didn't particularly like that I was setting off to the woods on a weekend, which might mean it would be crowded. In this sensibility, I share something in common with McCandless and Treadwell.

When I arrived, it was as I feared. The parking lot was packed. The metal of the cars gleamed sharply in the intense spring sunlight, and there was not a single open parking spot. I mulled about whether I should wait until someone returned from their outing and left the parking lot, but then again, this wasn't exactly the post office and that might take all day. I could have driven a bit farther up the road and found another trailhead into the forest, but I didn't want to do that either. I finally decided to do something I hardly ever do, which is to say to hell with the rules, and parked my car outside of the designated parking area, next to a snowdrift between a big spruce tree and a small transformer station. I grabbed my backpack, locked the door responsibly, and off I went.

I followed the same paths that I had on my previous expeditions, my backpack on my shoulders, my beanie in my hand. I could tell that my Iditarod boots and backpack had started conforming to my body and its rhythm because the creaking noises were fewer now. In behind the trees I could hear the *slip-slip* sound of skis gliding along hardened, late-winter ski tracks. I greeted folks on my right and left and smiled at everyone I passed.

When I got to the frozen lake, I met a man who wondered why I was walking when I could be on cross-country skis. "Why are you walking?" he asked, a question I had never thought I would be asked. He was one of those classic outdoor types: in his mid-sixties, unnaturally tanned for this time of year, hat pushed back on his forehead, thin skis, expensive clothes. *I walk therefore I am*, I might have replied, but instead I mumbled something about how I was taking pictures and so it's better to go on foot than to have to handle skis and poles. The man nodded, leaned over his poles, and skated off to the west. You might be one of those people with lots of savings in high-risk funds and success, I thought, but your style, old man, your somewhat too-quick tempo and the small signs of lost balance betray that time will eventually catch up, even with you.

I kept going. The deeper I ventured into the woods, the fewer people I encountered. I skirted the campsite without crossing it. I had decided that if I left tracks in the snow leading to the site, passing skiers like the man I'd just met might notice them, stop, and exclaim: "Look, a solitary hiker has been here on foot, on foot! And the tracks look fresh! Come on, let's go see where they lead!"

This was not a risk I was willing to take. In addition, now that the light would remain until long into the evening, there was no need to rush. I had left my tent at home this time and was planning to sleep directly on the snow. As such, there was no camp to set up. I could simply return at the end of the day when it had started to get dark and all the skiers were hopefully on their way home.

March is a transitional month. Or, more correctly: March marks the start of a transitional period that lasts until the light and warmth have displaced the darkness and cold for good, and strictly speaking it isn't until July that this really happens in Norway. In March, the old and the new seasons battle for dominion. One minute you're freezing, the next you're too hot. The temperature change between sunlight and shade is significant. It's not unusual for it to get up to seventy degrees in the middle of the day and down to subzero temperatures at night. If March were to be given a clinical diagnosis, it would have to be bipolar. My family's old motto of *Never trust the month of March* is therefore not very wide of the mark.

Three days had passed since the spring equinox, the time when the sun stays as long above the horizon as it does below it. In February, the increasing light was the only visible sign that time had passed since January. Now, the snowdrifts had melted on the south-facing slopes even if thigh-high snow still remained in places where it was flat. Under the thin layer of fresh snow, the ice was brown and porous, and beneath the spruce trees it was covered by a blanket of small brown needles.

I decided to hike in a different direction than I'd gone previously. A loop that I'd planned ahead of time, which was supposed to bring me back to the big lake where the mouth of the river opened up. I wanted to sit and keep a lookout for rising trout. Maybe it would be too early, but in any case it would be a nice spot to take a break, and there's nothing better than flowing water for the eyes to rest upon. If you ever come across an old campsite in the woods, chances are it is down near the edge of a lake or river or pond. And if you happen to see someone sitting there, chances are they are looking out toward the water, never in the opposite direction. The reason is at least partly practical, seeing as we need water to quench our thirst. But I think there's another, aesthetic explanation: we are drawn to the water because it is pleasant to look at. Maybe it's as simple as that. Maybe there is something anchored deep down in our biology that always pushes us to choose the open water instead of the dark, gloomy forest.

There were animal tracks everywhere. They led every which way, crisscrossing here and there, birds and mammals, big and small, paw or hoof marks in a cheerful blend. Moose and roe deer and rabbits. Most likely also foxes. Mice and squirrels and other scampering animals. There were bird markings wherever I looked: scrapings from winged struggles in the snow and from small, thin feet tiptoeing around lightly. Everything signaled that traffic was now afoot in the woods, a movement in nature that I hadn't previously seen. Territory to be defended. A potential mate to be courted. The stillness of winter would soon be replaced by an almost manic level of activity, because that's what life is like at this latitude where the winter is long and the climate subarctic. The brief span of time at a creature's disposal must be used to its fullest in order to pass along one's genes or to simply survive.

Arriving at the mouth of the river, I took out my food. Then I shaped the snow into a comfortable chair with a back-rest and arm supports and covered it with pine branches. I didn't see any trout rising, but along the edge of the ice on the opposite side of the river, two white-throated dippers were playing. I sat and watched these black-and-white birds that seem to pass their entire lives in the margin where water meets land. The water's edge is the zone of the white-throated dipper. Here it has all it needs to fully live as a dipper. The movement of the two birds was spasmodic: they flitted back and forth along the edge of the ice. One minute plunging down, the next bursting up again. They burst up onto the ice the way I've seen penguins do it on TV. They were obviously catching whatever was drifting along with the current. I assumed it must be midge larvae, tiny insects that hatch in the water all year long regardless of the temperature. The only thing a midge requires to hatch is open water. And here there was open water in abundance.

At a quarter past six, the sun went down. The evening sky was pale blue, almost white. The light grew slowly dimmer and the temperature dropped, but the two white-throated dippers kept at it along the bank. Plunging in and bursting back out, diving into the freezing river water and jaunting along the edge of the ice. Into the water, out again, into the water, out again.

The ice began to boom, and there was a cracking sound at the mouth of the river whenever new ice formed. It was a bit sad, in a way, since the project—that of forming new ice—was a futile one. The warmth of the new season would win in the end, but the water itself could not know that. It was simply doing what it does, following the laws of physics and changing form whenever temperatures reached a certain point. Whether it was spring or fall, it was all the same to the water. Eventually, it became too dark to make out the dippers along the edge of the ice, but I could still hear them, cackling away with their intense medley of light chirps and darker croaks.

I put on my backpack and began the climb toward the campsite. It wasn't hard to see ahead of me, even without a headlamp. The snow illuminated the scene, and soon enough the stars would come out and further light up the sky. There would be a full moon in three or four days. When I arrived at the point where I had to turn off from the logging road, I clambered up to the top of the snowbank. From there, I leaped off as far as I possibly could and landed in the dip beneath a large spruce tree. What a strange sight that must have been, I thought, if anyone had been there to see it. I had to crawl beneath the lowest branches of the tree right up next to the trunk and, after a small struggle, was able to scramble out the other side. After that, I trudged through the thigh-deep snow to reach the campsite. Perhaps this was a strange method of getting there, but the advantage was that I could sleep tight knowing that no cross-country skiers would see my tracks and decide to follow them. I wanted to be left alone. Especially since I would be sleeping without a tent, totally unprotected and exposed to my surroundings.

The campsite was untouched. I cut spruce branches which I then spread out on the snow in the exact spot where my tent had been in February. I stacked them in two layers and made sure the branches lay so that the curved part pointed upward. In that way, they would offer me a tiny bit of bounce and my bed would feel softer. Finally, I unrolled my sleeping pad and spread my sleeping bag out on top. After that, I reluctantly took off my shell jacket, microfiber jacket, and snow pants, stuffed them all into my backpack and crept down into the sleeping bag wearing nothing but my wool long johns, a sweater, socks, and a beanie.

Before I fell asleep, I tried to read *Into the Wild* by the light of my headlamp. Nothing else was visible other than the pages of my book. The woods around me were a black, oblique wall, and only the gods know what was lurking in there behind me.

I really like the film about Chris McCandless's life, even though it leaves out some of the nuance that is present in the book. In the film, he rebels against his parents and against the profit-oriented consumer society around him. Society is the enemy and the individual is the hero. The story is shaped like a romantic tragedy meant to leave the viewer feeling a blend of awe, grief, envy, and self-shame. Krakauer's book, by contrast, is bursting with perspective. He compares Chris McCandless to other, similar explorers. There are many such figures in the young history of the US; many of them have been drawn to Alaska like a magnet. It represents "the last frontier," the only place where it is still possible to live freely, as Thoreau described it in *Walden*:

> *I went to the Woods because I wished to live deliberately, to front only the essential facts of life, and see if I could not learn what it had to teach, and not, when I came to die, discover that I had not lived.*

Naturally, Chris McCandless was a reader of Thoreau. While living in the bus on the Stampede Trail, he even paraphrased the famous quote:

> <u>Deliberate living</u>: *Conscious attention to the basics of life, and a constant attention to your immediate environment and its concerns (...) all true meaning resides in the personal relationship to a phenomenon, what it means to you.*

It soon became clear that reading was an extremely impractical undertaking. It required me to hold the book up in front of my face, and in order to do that, at least one arm had to be sticking out of my sleeping bag at all times. Every time I finished a page and needed to turn to the next one, I had to extract my other arm from the sleeping bag to do so and this arrangement proved to be very cold after a while. I shoved the book and my headlamp and glasses down into my sleeping bag, cinched it over my head, pulled my beanie down tightly over my face, and lay thinking about other explorers I've read about.

Richard Proenneke is a man I respect. He spent long portions of his life all alone in the Alaskan wilderness at a place he christened Twin Lakes. The first time he went there was at the end of the sixties. Proenneke was a mechanic and carpenter by trade. He was a practical man in every way. He built his own notched-log cabin, which is still standing as an attraction for hikers today. Proenneke filmed his activities. He filmed himself building the cabin, paddling in the canoe, whittling various tools out of wood, or just sitting outside his cabin looking at the lake. The narrative voice is rough and plain. Proenneke never talks about himself as the focal point of the expedition. His attention is always turned outward, toward his surroundings. He speaks about what he has to get done, when he has to do it, and how. The cabin must be readied for the first snowfall, the notches must be made like this or like that. Over and over again, he emphasizes the importance of taking one's time, of never straining to speed up the task. He rarely talks about other people, nor does he mention his political or personal motivations for living the way he does.

I had also watched a film about a man who set out to live completely alone in northern Canada, relying only on the food he could get from the land for one hundred days in the summer of 2009. This man filmed himself too, and the result was a three-episode documentary TV series that was aired on the National Geographic Channel. The man was, in many ways, the polar opposite of Proenneke.

The film starts in an aircraft on its way across the barren wilderness. The man is filming his own face. He is excited and says he's done a lot of things like this before, that he's even climbed Mount Everest. But this—going alone for a hundred days in the wilderness—he can't be too sure how it is going to pan out.

The aircraft lets him out at a particular spot, lifts off again, and flies away. The man keeps the camera on his own face, which is smiling and ecstatic. Already at this early point in the film it's obvious that he is thinking more about the media version of himself than anything else, and that this film is going to be seen by hundreds of thousands of people.

While Proenneke's attention is turned outward, toward his surroundings and the practical work at hand, the man in the TV series almost always focuses inward, on himself. He is a kind of narcissist in the wilderness, and that certainly cannot be easy. He repeats ad nauseam that there are bears in the area, and that he is all alone. The first day he paddles out onto the lake with a fishing rod. He quickly catches a grayling that he prepares and eats for supper. From that point on, everything goes downhill. He cries into the camera, says he misses people—"someone to hold and hug" and to talk to. Two weeks later, he is complaining about how hungry he is. This point seems odd, since he has a fishing rod and is at the edge of a gigantic lake in Canada. He shoots a porcupine and a few squirrels. He waits for the salmon to come upriver. He never films himself fishing. Slowly he grows more and more emaciated, and slowly more listless. The only thing that still seems to interest him is himself and his own condition. After fifty days, he gives up. He sends an sos signal over the radio and when the seaplane lands on the lake a short while later, he films himself crying and hugging the pilot.

Richard Proenneke had planned to live in his cabin at Twin Lakes for two years. He stayed for thirty. When he turned eighty-two, he moved to live with his brother in California, where he lived out the rest of his life. He died in 2003.

I slept the entire night outside and didn't wake up until my alarm rang at four. It's hard to describe the disharmony of that moment, an electronic tone ringing in the middle of the vast, black silence. But I'm a civilized being, after all, and I wanted to see the sunrise. My sleeping bag had a thin layer of frost on it, but I hadn't been cold in the night. I stuffed my things into my backpack by the light of my headlamp. I lit a fire and made coffee. Then I walked home, slowly and in silence. I looked for moose, encouraged by my experience in February. The sky was still populated by the twinkling stars. The spruce trees lined the logging road like unmoving shadows. It felt as if I were walking through a tunnel or sitting in a spaceship on the way toward new galaxies. Every shape my eyes fell upon looked like it could be a moose in the feeble light of morning, but whenever I stopped to get a closer look, it was always only a tree or a rock or a large overturned root. A fox sauntered across an open meadow below the road. It ran easily and without a care. When it saw me, it stopped and lifted its head. After that it was gone in a flash between the spruces. I did not see any moose this time. Disappointed, I ambled down the final hills thinking this would be the last I'd see of winter this year.

By the time I reached the parking lot, it was fully light out. The songbirds were awake and twittering, and the sun was peeking up over the tall ridges in the east. The parking lot was empty except for one car off to the side, which was pressed into the snowbank between a spruce tree and a transformer station. Ah, so no one but me had stayed out in the woods last night, I thought, satisfied. I started the car, praising the invention of the heater, and turned the nose of my car toward the city and all its inhabitants.

# PART II

# SPRING

# APRIL

---

"Few things are harder to visualize than that a cold, snow-bound landscape, so marrow chillingly quiet and lifeless, will, within mere months, be green and lush and warm, quivering with all manner of life, from birds warbling and flying through the trees to swarms of insects hanging in scattered clusters in the air. Nothing in the winter landscape presages the scent of sun-warmed heather and moss, trees bursting with sap and thawed lakes ready for spring and summer (...) It is not there, it does not exist, everything is white and still, and if the silence is broken it is by a cold wind or a lone crow caw-cawing. But it is coming...it is coming..."

**KARL OVE KNAUSGÅRD**, *MY STRUGGLE, PART I*

THE DIFFERENCE BETWEEN spending a night in the woods by yourself and spending a night with someone else is so enormous that it's almost impossible to exaggerate. It doesn't matter if it's only one other person, or twenty. Alone or not alone, that is the question. The choice of company or no company affects everything down to the most minute detail, but the most important thing is this: when you are alone, speaking ceases. You don't make any noise yourself, other than the noise created by your feet as they touch the forest floor. And you instinctively curtail as much of this noise as you can. When you are alone, you steal through the woods without realizing it, particularly after it has gotten dark. You don't want to disturb anything, and you also don't want to be discovered. That's just the way it is. Tuned in at this level of caution, you thus see and hear more of what is taking place around you. I don't need to worry about exaggerating when I say that you see and hear almost everything when you are alone in the woods and almost nothing when you are with others.

It was a mild, sun-filled day in the second half of April. It was a weekend. I was outside our four-person house with my backpack at my feet. Along the side of the road, the yellow grass from last season had been joined by one or two green blades, and on the trees, the buds had grown to a noticeable size over the past few days. The asphalt was dry and bright and it gave off a wonderful warmth. From surrounding gardens, I could hear the sounds of laughter and children's voices, the low hum of adult voices, the tinkling of coffee in cups, the characteristic creak of elastic stretching whenever children's feet came down on trampolines. I was standing on the threshold of a new season, the spring, the most celebrated of them all. The metaphor for everything positive in the world: birth and love and hope and luck and new chances to replace the wasted ones.

This fourth leg of the micro-expedition stood out from the three previous ones in two significant ways, and I was, to tell the truth, skeptical about both of them. It was my own fault, but as I waited, I could no longer remember why I had thrown in these two changes now that I was gearing up. The first change was that I had invited along a hiking companion. A photographer named Kristian who would take photos and film, and in that way document this little event. I don't have anything against Kristian in the slightest— he is a great guy in every respect—but there's no getting around the fact that he is a human being, and up until now the entire purpose had been to remove myself from human beings. The second change was that, for the first time, my expedition would lead to a different destination than the small glacial pond with the campsite. April is the month during which the wood grouse carry out their ancient courtship ritual, and one of the goals of this particular stage was to witness it. A wood grouse or a black grouse or both, it didn't matter which. We would take whatever we could get.

The campsite at the pond was not a good spot for observing grouse, so we decided it would be best to venture farther north in the forest to a location known for such rituals.

As I soaked up the spring sunshine, I couldn't help but feel annoyed at myself for having initiated these two changes, and perhaps particularly the latter one. The entire point of this micro-expedition was *not* to have the kind of goals that grand expeditions boast of. Where others charge straight ahead, I wanted to meander in circles, and in that I had done uncommonly well during the winter stages. But then, in a momentary lapse of attention, what had I done but gone and forgotten the whole point and suddenly got it into my head that observing the courtship rituals of wood grouse should be the goal for April.

The logic made absolutely no sense to me now as I stood waiting for Kristian. He phoned to tell me he would be late. When he finally drove up, a big man in a little car, his entire countenance showed his bad conscience. I like to imagine it was because we were headed to the woods, because he had an instinctive respect for what lay ahead of him—and because he realized that if there is one thing that avid forest-goers cannot abide, it is people who are late.

This thought cheered me up considerably. We packed our gear in the trunk and drove out of Oslo, northward, through the suburbs along Highway 4. As we drove, I expounded on courtship rituals and the typical sites. I said:

*Sparse forest, preferably pine, or else spruce, preferably old growth, or else new growth, usually swampy, but not necessarily, usually near open water, but not necessarily a must. Now is the best time of year, but it depends on the temperatures. The wood grouse arrives at the mating site in the evening, it sleeps in the trees, the ritual begins in the early morning hours, we will have to camouflage ourselves, and remain totally silent, pay attention.*

Kristian apparently believed I knew what I was talking about, even though I didn't. Kristian seemed in general to have an overly heightened respect for my competence as an expedition leader, and so I decided not to mention the part that I had only spent a total of three nights outside on my own, at least in this current phase of my life. I almost felt I deserved to bask in my unearned reputation for a day and a night.

Kristian said he was looking forward to spending a night in the woods, but he wasn't sure about his gear. He had good shoes and a solid pair of hiking pants, but only a cotton pullover and a sleeping bag that looked alarmingly old and thin. I didn't mention that, in all likelihood, it was going to be a very cold night. The fact that there were no clouds in the middle of the day meant that the temperatures were going to drop as soon as the sun went down because all of the warmth escapes into the sky when there's no insulating cloud cover. Kristian's sleeping bag was too thin. As soon as we packed it in the car, I knew he would be in for an uncomfortable night under the open sky. But it was too late to do anything about it, and he probably wouldn't die.

We veered off the highway and continued on a forest ser-
vice road. The road sloped steadily upward, and at the top
of the hill, after gaining 500 to 1,000 feet of elevation from
the valley floor, it flattened out. The agricultural landscape
beneath us stretched to the north and the west as far as the
eye could see. Farming season was underway down there;
it was a patchwork of fields, big and small, brown and green.
And mountains far off in the distance, bluish, enveloped in
a haze of heat.

The road stopped at a barrier next to a large parking lot.
We parked the car, shouldered our packs, and began to walk.
The gravel road was soft and muddy. The ground frost must
have melted only recently, as the sides of the road were still
covered in snow. After half an hour, we left the logging
road and followed a path that was barely visible between
the trees' naked branches. The trail had once been an old
cart track. According to the map, it led down toward an
area with three small ponds and one large, interconnected
peat bog. It was the perfect playground for the birds. The
wood grouse in the surrounding wooded areas. The black
grouse in the open marshes. Because we didn't have a lot of
distance to cover, we were able to take our time. We kept
our eyes peeled for anemones but we didn't see any. The
snow on the north-facing slopes was still piled deep, though
it was coarse and porous now. We were happy and in high
spirits, the way people often are when tramping through the
woods on a mild spring day—and people who are happy and
in high spirits have a tendency to talk and jabber quite a lot.

The more noise we made, the less noise the forest around us made. The more we spoke, the less attention we paid. We checked the map. We had not been paying enough attention and had walked too far. We turned around and walked back. Then we split off from the path and moved down toward the valley floor, where we hoped to find the three small ponds and the large peat bog.

We clambered through a thicket of young birch trees. The terrain flattened out and we emerged into a more open area dominated by pine. This is wood grouse territory, I thought, peering vigilantly to my right and left. Kristian was walking directly behind me. We began to speak in whispers. There was no reason to think we might chance across a wood grouse now, in the middle of the day, but I enjoyed sneaking around in that manner. In addition, my many years as a fly-fisherman had taught me that you can never really know what to expect from wildlife. It's not uncommon for animals to suddenly do something that they otherwise never do, and at this time of year the forest birds were so full of hormones they almost bordered on madness. Anything could happen, and it was best to be prepared. The fact that Kristian was walking behind me carrying his video camera also had a certain impact on me, causing me to lurk about as gracefully and nonchalantly as I possibly could, which reminded me of the self-conscious behavior of the man in the TV series.

I said to Kristian that the plan was to select a few promising spots that we would return to at dawn the following morning. That was my plan, and when you are looking for a certain type of terrain in this manner, it's often the case that you think you see it everywhere. Every square inch seems like it could be a promising spot, and it was no different for me. We took note of the various locations and decided on where we would return to in the morning.

But now, we were hungry. We wanted to get out of the dense tree cover. We wanted to light a campfire and find a good campsite, but just in that moment we stumbled across the skeleton of a large animal and stood there for a good while, wordlessly staring down at it. The skeleton had long, sharp canine teeth and the body was about three feet long. The skeleton was complete. It lay on its side, curled up and somewhat sunken into the forest floor. This skeleton had once been a mammal. Maybe it had been wandering around on these cart tracks when it slowly began to feel its energy waning and then, in quiet wonderment, decided to lie down for a while to rest. And that is where its life ended. The hide and flesh, skin and tendons and entrails, had all been eaten or decayed, but the skeleton had remained, who knows for how long, without anyone having seen it. "We are the first ones," said Kristian. "Is it a wolf?" I replied that I didn't have a clue, but it was too big to be a fox and the shape of its head did not look like a lynx. It couldn't be a wolverine either, so then it would have to have been a wolf or a dog. We decided it must have been a dog. The remains of what had been a dog now lay there, and someone must once have missed it.

We stared at the skeleton for a long time. Then we tore ourselves away and continued on through the woods.

In the 1990s, the word "multitasking" entered the lexicon of the Norwegian workplace. Like a lot of other things that were incorporated into the workplace in the '90s—open-concept offices, scooters in the hallways, suits with tennis shoes, and teambuilding—multitasking was openly embraced by modern Norwegian business leaders. Multitasking means doing several things at the same time. And if multitasking is in fact necessary, it implies that every single employee at every single moment has so many different things to do that the entire organization will collapse if they aren't multitasking. It is thus essential that they reply to emails while on the toilet, talk on the phone while filing travel expenses, scarf down lunch while reviewing the meeting minutes.

Multitasking presupposes a particular cognitive ability, and this ability is called *simultaneous capacity*. How good you are at multitasking depends on your level of simultaneous capacity. That psychologists and brain researchers doubt whether it is even in fact possible for the human brain to handle two simultaneous thoughts doesn't seem to have the slightest effect on modern business leaders. The way I understand it, the general perception is that the brain cannot simultaneously hold two ideas, but it can shift focus very rapidly from one topic to another and back again. Simultaneous capacity is thus synonymous with a lack of concentration, which is the opposite of deeper understanding. The result is that we have a lot of people doing a whole bunch of things, with none of them doing any single thing really well.

Multitasking could be a keyword for nature in April, but in the wild this manic activity level is neither illusory nor arrogant but vital for the earth's wild inhabitants. After months of hibernation, nature bursts forth in every direction. Places where only a few weeks ago everything seemed dead and quiet now teem with life. The cause is as simple as it is obvious. In northern latitudes like Norway or North America, everything has to take place within a short window of springtime weeks if new life is to gain enough strength before winter sets in. Multitasking is an absolute necessity for animals and birds and all lifeforms that call nature their home. In the wild, focusing on only one task at a time is like not paying attention and is the surest path to certain death. The wild inhabitants of the earth must find a mate, construct a residence, protect their property, keep competitors away, eat others, and avoid being eaten themselves. The idyll about the peacefulness of the woods is never more erroneous than in the spring. In fact, industry and chaos reign from sunup to sundown in a frenzy of intense activity, tight deadlines, ambitious entrepreneurial undertakings, quarrels about property rights, and shows of muscle. Beneath the surface of it all surges an endless sex drive, which is both at the root of most conflicts and the source for the perpetuation of life.

We continued our walk through the woods in complete silence. Perhaps it was the skeleton that quieted us; it had certainly left an impression on us. The result, in any case, was that the surrounding birdsong began to crescendo, or maybe it had been there the whole time but we had not noticed.

We trudged on in single file through the cacophony of new life. The streams of sunlight sliced through the open woodland and shimmered and gleamed on the damp forest floor. We arrived at the first pond, crossed the first peat bog, continued through a copse, and came out onto a larger bog that led out to another pond. In several places, the bog stretched a hundred feet or so from the edge of the pond to where the forest began. In the summer months this spot would be bursting with life, but for now the bog appeared to be lifeless. The bog was soggy in some spots and frozen in others. We found the perfect site for camping, a small rise in the midst of the bog adjacent to a cluster of birch trees. The ground there was drier and more solid. More importantly, the campsite was somewhat separated from the area where I was most certain the grouse would come. For all I knew, I could be totally wrong. Maybe we had chosen to settle down smack dab in the middle of the grouse ritual spot, but you have to take some risks in life, and we needed a campsite.

Kristian wanted to film me gathering firewood. Once again, I became the guy in the Canadian wilds. It was impossible not to put up a front. On film I wanted to come across as nonchalant, to appear as though every one of my actions was familiar and ordinary to me. I snapped off a few dry branches close to the trunk of an old, gnarled spruce tree. The branches were hard as nails and very thick, and they gave off a resounding crack when they finally snapped. One of the branches lashed my hand. Blood spilled from the deep gash and I could feel the intense pain down my hand, but I acted like it was nothing. "Look at that guy," future viewers might exclaim, "he's got blood oozing out of his hand and he doesn't even notice! Now there's a man who's spent a lot of time in the woods!"

Out on the bog, the afternoon crept slowly toward evening. The sun lingered above the hill and the temperature was warm and comfortable. We settled in and perfected our campsite. A pile of dry wood was stacked and ready to go for the campfire. We collected enough fresh spruce branches to make a padded bed platform for each of us. We placed our sleeping pads on top and then our sleeping bags over the pads. We had not brought a tent.

After getting our sleeping situation in order, we lit a large fire, sat down, and there we remained. We ate and talked, drank whiskey, and had a splendid time. Kristian was cheerful and interesting, curious about everything around him, ready to learn about this or that. He wanted to know why I had decided to undertake this micro-expedition, why I wanted to go alone, and what kind of gear I needed. What was the most important thing? What was the least important? I answered as best as I could, and I thought maybe it wasn't so ridiculous that I had invited him on this outing after all. If I'd been alone, I would be sitting in complete silence, my ears alert. Then I would finally creep into my sleeping bag and long for morning to come.

At eleven p.m., we let the fire die down and each of us settled into his own sleeping bag. At that same moment, two cranes flew over the pond. They came from the south, and the noise of their flight preceded them—the ruffle of their large wings and heavy bodies. And then there they were, gray and obscure and ghostlike, like two souls flickering in the dusk.

All evening long, Kristian had expressed admiration for my orange sleeping bag and also skepticism regarding his own blue one. He'd owned it for several years, he told me, as is often the case with sleeping bags. You get one from your parents when you are in your early teens, around the time of your confirmation, and it accompanies you into adulthood. Over the last few decades, sleeping bags have evolved considerably, with the result that a product that was adequate in the 1980s no longer makes the cut. However, Kristian reported that his sleeping bag was surprisingly warm, and here I must admit that I smiled to myself as he told me. When you've been sitting around a fire for several hours with whiskey pumping through your veins, of course everything is going to feel cozy and warm as you nod comfortably off to sleep. But the moment you fall asleep, your body will start to cool down, and because the whiskey is running warm in your blood, it is going to take longer to notice just how cold and uncomfortable you are and to wake up. Once awake, the feeling of icy cold is completely different than what most people mean when they say they feel cold. I've experienced a similar feeling many times before, half-awake and shivering through long nights in a tent alongside my warm and cozy, snoring hiking buddies.

Perhaps Kristian would not freeze to death out there on the bog, but he was certainly in for an uncomfortable night. There was nothing I could do. Maybe he would be of hardier stock than me, I thought. After all, people's ability to retain heat seems to vary quite widely, and I am always one of the first people to get cold.

We lay in our sleeping bags and chatted for a while and then we said our goodnights. From the hills that rose up around the bog on every side now rose noises. Creeping and crawling in the woods, cracking and creaking and rustling and peeping. A vast system of infinite proportions was astir following the long winter and there was not a moment to waste.

I fell asleep and woke up several times. I lay in my sleeping bag peering out into the spring night. The darkness was not as dense as it had been in the winter. I could make out the contours of the hill across the pond, like a roughly pixelated photograph. From the sound of Kristian's moaning, it seemed he had fallen asleep. I nodded off again and didn't wake up until my phone began to ring from somewhere deep in my sleeping bag.

It was four a.m. It was still dark out. My sleeping bag was covered in a layer of frost, but I didn't feel cold. It was probably only about fifteen degrees outside, the moon hung big and white above a ridge in the west, the coals in the campfire had gone out. I propped myself up on my elbows. Kristian was lying on his side in his blue sleeping bag with his back toward me. I spoke to him, quietly at first and then louder. He started to moan. "I'm fucking freezing," he said. "I haven't slept for a single goddamn second!" He looked so spent that I decided now wasn't the time to crack jokes. I could empathize with what he was going through. We lit a fire and it helped with the cold. We ate breakfast and packed our gear. It began to get lighter. We spoke in low tones. Kristian said the first thing he was going to do when we got back to the city was to buy a new sleeping bag. I agreed that was a good idea. Then we picked up our packs and began retracing our steps from the previous day.

I have never seen the grouse courtship ritual as an adult, but I am inclined to believe I witnessed it with my grandfather when I was a child. He often observed it and liked to tell us about it, and maybe I've mixed up one of his tales with my real-life memories. My grandfather said: "Stand totally still until the wood grouse begins making its characteristic noise. At that point, it has entered into a kind of trance and you can take a few steps forward to get closer." Kristian walked ahead of me. Every ten yards or so we stopped to listen. There was no noise in the woods, nothing to indicate an impending mating ritual. We felt a little silly walking there, like two posers with only each other as spectators. Each step on the bog crunched underfoot. The marsh had frozen overnight and it was impossible to move without making a sound. It was like creeping around on a sea of dry crackers, and in that moment I felt I'd lost faith in ever seeing a grouse on this outing.

New ice covered the surface of the pond and two white wagtails, the tiny migratory birds that symbolize the first signs of spring, were walking on it. They were the first wagtails I'd seen that year, and they flitted here and there, turning their heads, twitching their tails. Some portion of this bird is always in motion: it can never hold completely still. "A wagtail ritual, that's something," I whispered to Kristian.

It was completely light out now. We continued half-heartedly, fully at a loss about whether we were on track to find anything at all. The longer we walked, the less we cared about the noise we were making. By the time we got back to the dead dog, we had long since given up any hope of seeing a grouse, even though neither of us had said it out loud. We took one last look at the skeleton sunk into the forest floor. And then we headed for the parking lot, chattering the entire way.

# MAY

## CIVILIZATION AND
## ITS DISCONTENTS

―――――

"When spring came (...) there were no problems
except where to be happiest. The only thing that
could spoil a day was people and if you could keep
from making engagements, each day had no limits."

**ERNEST HEMINGWAY,** *A MOVEABLE FEAST*

FOR THOSE WHO thrive in their own company, the
month of May can be a challenge. It is the period of
great collisions. It's the day for going to find lilies-of-
the-valley, but then it turns out that your nephew George's
confirmation falls on the same day that the flowers bloom.
The first mayflies are hatching and just then your family
receives an invitation to coffee and cake with the John-
sons down the road. The grouse courtship ritual has to be

cancelled because your Uncle John shows up with a fist-
ful of tickets to the amusement park and everyone has to
come along.

That's how May is. It is a month so chock-full of events,
both in nature and culture, that it's impossible to avoid conflict. And nature always loses. To amble about aimlessly in
the woods alone is considered neither a socially acceptable
nor constructive activity, at least not in my country and
maybe not in any other country. There is little empathy in
western culture for the kinds of individuals who might prefer huddling alone in a small dome tent to attending a large
garden party with fifty other human beings. The urge to be
alone is not taken seriously.

My dream of creating a temporary refuge, twelve days
for myself alone, was not met with nearly as many obstacles
in any of the other months as it was in May. There was too
much of everything, and I reacted with anger and frustration. May is the most celebrated of all the months of the year,
the subject of countless poems and ballads—more so than
any other month. Without exception, such songs tend to be
about how mild and beautiful everything is, about the birds
building their nests and the cuckoo cuckooing. But what
good is all of that if you aren't there to see it?

Throughout the winter, life had been easy. There were
hardly any appointments to keep, and the few events on my
calendar took place on a weekly basis. They were routine;

they didn't require any action on my part other than to remember they were there. Once we managed to get past New Year's Eve, there came a period of almost one hundred ordinary days in a row, as monotonous and straightforward as a quiet, snow-covered meadow.

The calm settled in. I was in my element. Each day was like the next, and since the changes in nature are so minute with each passing day at this time of year, they were easy to follow. There was either more snow or less snow on any given day. Pink sunrises over the rooftops in the east, or else a white, featureless sky. A new kind of bird showing up at the feeder. An icy wind from the north.

Daylight had lengthened by four minutes since the solstice.

Every winter for as long as I can remember, I have told myself: now you have to pay attention, you have to take note of the details, preserve those tiny moments that you only have now and never again. They didn't exist yesterday and they will be gone tomorrow. Every winter this is what I tell myself, but when the spring arrives, slurping down my attention more than any other season, I miss them. I fall into a slumber of sorts, I am no longer able to see, and one day rolls into another until I suddenly find myself sitting on the streetcar feeling vexed because it's too hot.

This year was no exception. For the first half of May, I had a frustrating amount of work to do. There had been delays, deadlines began to loom, new projects popped up.

I was in a constant state of irritation over the fact that we are required to spend our entire lives working at jobs and just how meaningless some of these jobs can seem at times, my own job included.

My email inbox was overflowing with messages, almost all of them demanding something from me. They were about new projects, meeting locations, dress codes, and scope of responsibility. I printed out spreadsheet attachments full of dates that I promptly entered into my calendar. The danger of forgetting something is heightened in May, and I hate forgetting things. I was agitated, I felt trapped, and I got annoyed as I always do when I think about how gleeful some people are about making plans. About how they insist on celebrating every conceivable little occasion to death, together with groups of other people. I could go crazy knowing that entire days are swallowed up in such a manner, because the events occurring in nature at the very same time are over before you know it and then you have to wait an entire year before they come around again, and when they do, you know you are going to find yourself in the same boat as the previous year, with the same danger of being consumed by society.

May is the month during which the flurry and fleeting nature of life is most apparent to me. Not September and October, which many people like to point to as a metaphor, but May. For me, it is the month that most clearly reveals just how brief life is, that nothing lasts forever, and that every-thing one day will reach its end.

The first week in May was particularly bad. I wanted to go to the woods. Some of my friends had already been out fly-fishing and caught their first trout. I hoped the ice on the pond near my campsite would be melted by now and that the temperature would soon rise to the level required for the mayflies to hatch. But then there was the question of my work duties. And the family. Everything that, when lumped together, I refer to as "culture" in this book.

I typed frenetically on my computer, and every time I took a break I pored over my calendar. I was looking for breathing spaces in the bloated days, small moments in which to get everything done, and every time the only moveable variable was the number of hours I could sleep at night.

I therefore introduced a new routine in which I woke up at five o'clock every morning, worked until six thirty, and then got the rest of my family up and running with all our normal morning rituals. After the others had left for work, day care, and school, I dove back into my job, and in that way, I worked out that I would have seven-and-a-half hours of work, or one extra standard working day per week. I felt irritable and impetuous and prone to snap at the tiniest offenses. And I got tired. I was following the schedule of a Japanese salaryman while earning next to nothing. My one-man business was probably the least successful entrepreneurial idea in the world. The whole thing made me furious.

I yelled at the kids when they asked if we could drive to school or day care in the morning instead of walking. Maybe it was raining lightly outside. Or maybe there was a harsh spring wind. I told them that regardless we would be walking to school because driving a car pollutes the earth. They argued that shoes pollute the earth too: they leave traces of rubber on the asphalt. "Consider Jan Baalsrud, our national hero from the Second World War!" I yelled at them. "He cut off his own toes and skied all the way to Sweden with the Germans at his heels! And you kids can't even walk a quarter of a mile to school in sixty-degree weather?"

I have a tendency to invoke Jan Baalsrud whenever my kids refuse to walk somewhere. Baalsrud is a frequent houseguest of sorts in our home, and they have long since grown immune to his dramatic fate. I argued and argued. Day in and day out. It was my fault, of course.

May 17, the Norwegian national holiday drew near. My Japanese sleeping regimen lasted for two weeks before I gave it up. I was suffering from a lack of sleep and stress and a general malaise. I would sit inside, typing away all day, every day. Soon I was the pastiest man in the neighborhood, and my joints and muscles ached, especially when I sat down to work at five in the morning. Some people suggested I might have a vitamin-D deficiency—since I was inside all the time, they said. I replied, yes, maybe, and thought about Sigmund Freud, the Austrian doctor who is best known for developing psychoanalysis.

In a small book called *Das Unbehagen in der Kultur* (literally "the uneasiness in civilization" but translated into English with the title: *Civilization and Its Discontents*), Freud claims there will always be a fundamental conflict between the individual and society. For society to function, and to keep things from falling apart completely, a pact of sorts must exist between citizens, particular guidelines around what one can and cannot do. An individual must suppress multiple natural drives in order to coexist peacefully with others, among these the so-called death drive, aggression, which is what comprises all that is opposed to culture. Most individuals are able to do this fairly well, Freud says, but for some this suppression can lead to neurosis and psychosis. Typical Freud, he always manages to drag in neurosis and psychosis. I read this book while studying at university many years ago and I honestly remember very little about it. But I like the title, and this was what was on my mind in May. Relax, I told myself as I hunched over my keyboard. It's nothing but civilization and its discontents. You're neither neurotic nor psychotic; you're only a person who'd prefer to be out hiking in the woods.

Days passed. I was a sullen and inattentive pen-pusher, and yet I was able to notice something about the spring. The first time I took note of the warmth was on Tuesday, May 7. Suddenly the temperatures were summerly, and the air so mild that the kids tore off their sweaters and ran out into the garden in nothing but t-shirts, shouting: "Spring!" The following day it was cold again. It felt like the previous day hadn't happened, and it continued like this until, on the afternoon of May 16, I was out in the garden putting up a garden party tent with my good neighbor Dagur. Suddenly and without warning, a mild breeze wafted through the garden. It was so different, this breeze, that the body reacted instinctively. Two men stood there on the grass, fiddling with bracing wires and tent poles; the breeze blew in, and they let the bracing wires slack and lifted their heads at almost exactly the same moment, as if they were two grazing roe deer that had both just heard a strange sound from the nearby cluster of trees.

This is the turning point, I thought. Right now, in this very moment, summer has arrived.

A few hours later, warm air had replaced the cold. The thermometer rose from below fifty degrees to above seventy. In several parts of the country there were soon reports of record highs, and I read online that it had even reached eighty degrees in northern Norway, which around here is considered warm.

When I finally had a lull in my schedule and could think about going to the woods again, there were of course only a few days left in the month. I was in a bad mood. I knew I should probably stay home because there was still so much work to be done, and I had a meeting in the city at eight the next morning. I was worried the outing would have to be severely truncated, so I decided that to do it right, I would leave at dawn one morning, before anyone else had even woken up. In the worst case, I would have to return late that same evening, so it would not technically count as

an entire night spent outside, but at least it would be a day
in the woods.

It was still warm out, but dark clouds had pushed in from
the east. There wasn't any wind, but the weather was still
moody, muggy, and oppressive. The night before my trip, I
packed a light 32-liter backpack with only the bare essentials: tarp, sleeping pad, sleeping bag. One change of wool
long johns, a wool pullover, socks, and a thin pair of rain
pants. One package of crispbread, a tube of bacon-cheese,
two portions of freeze-dried dinner. A fly-fishing rod and
reel and a matchbox with a few flies in it. Before I went to
sleep, I checked the weather forecast. It predicted heavy rain
throughout the next day and into the night.

In an article published in the *Dagbladet* newspaper just
before Christmas of 2012, when I was finalizing the practical details of my micro-expedition, a professor of social
medicine named Per Fugelli wrote: *Don't be a number-1 on
the earth. Tend to your flock.* The article touched a nerve, and
the phrase was widely adopted throughout the country as
the sagest of advice.

By the time I embarked on my first, lonely, January night
in the woods, the idea that we need to stop being so indi-
vidualistic and care for those closest to us like we are all
part of a precious brood of chickens had become such a well-
established truth in Norwegian society that I felt a bit out
of touch with the zeitgeist. After all, I was traipsing alone
in the forest on a mission to realize a dream based on a

diametrically opposed need. Though my desire in no way felt like a case of aggression or Freudian death drive, I did feel somewhat like a deviant.

People who claim that "hanging out with friends" is their favorite pastime are the supreme beings of the modern era, optimally suited to a global context in which success is measured by how many friends you have or how vast your social network is. We are living in a time when people with the greatest social radius are held up as role models: the hubs of a network of influence that radiates like power lines or data streams. These influencers are everywhere and at every possible moment, in debates, at events, in interviews, at parties. If you follow them on social media, you quickly realize that they are able to participate effortlessly in ten or fifteen interactions at the same time, bouncing from criticizing someone to praising another in a matter of seconds.

There seems to be no subject on which these influencers don't have bold opinions—even the topic of outdoor recreation. And even if having an opinion is very different from having an informed opinion, that doesn't always stop them. I once saw the photo of a well-known Norwegian man alongside a newspaper article with the headline: LOVES TO FISH. There he was in full fishing gear, smiling. In his hands was a spinning rod, the kind that has a line suspended below the rod. Yet in the photograph the rod was turned so that the line was on top and, in addition, it had been mounted backwards. It was like looking at a skier standing atop of a pair of skis with the pointy tips behind him and the bindings pushed down into the snow, next to a headline claiming: LOVES TO SKI.

From an outsider's perspective, there seems to be nothing that such folks feel they haven't mastered, no single arena where they think they might not belong, and it makes me wonder: Do these people never spend any time by themselves? Are they never at home? Does someone else have to tend to their flock while they're giving all those TV interviews about how essential it is to tend to one's flock? Do they have to get a babysitter so they can spend time writing articles about how important it is to spend time with your children? Or do they perhaps imagine that *flock* refers to society at large, and therefore it's their duty to spend as much time as possible rubbing shoulders with society, so that the whole flock will see them and thereby feel a sense of security?

What about those of us who don't possess the same social capacity? What do we do when the flock grows too big, when we can no longer wrap our heads around it, when it eventually increases to include people we hardly know? What do we do when all of this social philanthropy threatens to take over, when we feel like we are drowning in well-intended invitations and overexaggerated empathy? What about those of us who enjoy being alone?

It was five a.m. Sharp white light was already pouring over the rooftops. I headed north with my backpack on. To the right was a large park. No one else was awake at five a.m., but seagulls circled the soccer fields in search of earthworms in the dewy grass. A taxi was parked next to a kiosk, its yellow cab light on. The driver was leaned back on the headrest and it looked as if he was sleeping. He had dark hair and a white shirt. Maybe he was from Iran. Maybe Afghanistan. Maybe he was an influencer who loved parties. Maybe he was a loner who preferred solitude. Perhaps something in the middle, but in any case, now he was asleep.

I kept walking, up, north, crossing roundabouts and medians; there were very few cars on the streets. I stopped at a blue bus stop shelter. A tiny path disappeared through the trees behind the stop. This is where the woods began. This was the edge of the Nordmarka forest. Oslo was spread out beneath me, only a few miles away. The city would soon stir: people would rush to their jobs, stop at the red lights, wait for green lights, drop kids off at day care, pick children up at after-school programs, telephone, email, jog, go shopping. The asphalt was wet and dark from the night's dew. There was a strong smell of damp earth and spruce. I crossed the street and turned around one final time. Then I slipped in between the trees and vanished into the woods, as if entering a magic spell in a fairy tale, as if I were a man from another time.

I carried around my fishing rod the whole day. It rained and then let up. Then it rained again. The birdsong was different than it had been in April, even though back then I hadn't imagined it could be possible. There was a wall of sound in the woods now, and the deciduous trees that had been naked in April were clothed in a greenish hue. In some spots, the leaves had almost begun to burst forth. In others, they were still contained in tiny buds on the trees. It had been a late spring. The hillsides were flanked with ten different shades of green, ranging from the palest birch trees to the darkest spruces.

I sauntered on and joined a trail I had never before taken. The forest floor was carpeted in wood anemones. Cowslips grew at the edges of small streams, and everywhere I heard the blackbird's characteristic chortle. Whenever I stopped to locate the sound, I almost always traced it to the top of the tallest spruce trees.

I continued down the path, checked my map, saw that it would in all likelihood lead me back to the old logging road and from there up to my usual campsite. There was no real reason to go back there on this spring day; I had only chosen that spot in December because the winter snow was so deep at the time and it was easy to get to. However, I could feel the desire to visit it again, especially since I had not gone in April, but also because I wanted to see if anything was rising in the little pond, and because, in some strange way, I missed this insignificant fleck of earth and woods and bog and pond.

By three in the afternoon, I had arrived. The weather had let up and there was even an occasional glimpse of blue sky. I took advantage of the opportunity to set up my tarp. A tarp is a rectangular piece of waterproof fabric with cords at all four corners and in the middle of each side. It can be suspended virtually anywhere and provides protection against wind and rain. It can be used as an extra rainfly or as a roof above your picnic area. It can be erected as a lean-to or as a tent. My tarp is the simplest and most versatile piece of outdoor equipment that I own. I drop mentions of it into all kinds of different conversations, and since it seems like so few people know what a tarp is, and since almost no one I know will ever need a tarp, I often receive strange looks. Still, I continue to mention tarps. There are worse topics to drone on about than tarps.

I decided I would use my tarp to fashion a tent. It was certainly going to start raining again, most likely very heavily, and so I thought the most sensible thing to do was to seal the sides as tightly as possible. I whittled a three-foot-long stick and pressed it twelve inches down into the soil. I found another stick that was only half as long and pushed it twelve inches deep as well. Then I pulled the tarp taut over the two sticks so that the top of each stick met the middle of each of the short ends. I pulled the tarp down on both side of the sticks, tightened it, and then fixed it to the ground with stakes. The result was a low, A-frame tent. There was no space to sit up inside, since it was important that the tarp reached the ground on all sides, and to do that I was forced to sacrifice some headroom. Still, there was more than enough room to lie down, and after all, that was what I would be using it for.

The tarp tent looked so inviting that I decided to try it out immediately. I crawled in and lay on my stomach on top of the sleeping pad. From this position, I boiled water on my stove and kept an eye on the pond. So far, no trout had shown themselves, but there weren't any insects to be seen either. When the water reached its boiling point, I turned off the gas. I opened the bag of freeze-dried backpacking food and dumped the hot water inside. Then I sealed the bag and left it to sit for five minutes to soak up the moisture and seasoning.

Freeze-dried backpacking food is expensive, so you should only bring it on trips when you either have a lot of other things to carry and need to limit the weight of your pack, or if you want to have as simple a meal as possible. But it tastes good, and if you believe the claims on the package, such food pumps you full of an almost inconceivable amount of energy for the rest of your day.

After supper, I lay under the tarp looking out at the pond. The clouds closed in again, and shortly after that it started to rain. The aftermath of my Japanese salaryman sleep regime and a long day in the woods had left me feeling exhausted. I wanted coffee but didn't have any water. As I lay there considering whether or not to drag myself down to the pond to get some, I fell asleep and the dilemma solved itself. When I woke up, the rain was coming down harder. I didn't know how long I'd been sleeping—maybe an hour? I heard the rain before I opened my eyes and I lay like that, with my eyes shut, listening to the rain increasing in strength. It's easy to be fooled by raindrops falling against a tarp;

it always sounds like a torrential downpour. But from what I could tell, a torrential downpour was not far from the truth. The rain hammered against the fabric. Water began to stream through the opening, not much, but enough to be uncomfortable.

At six, the rain subsided again. My elbows and thighs were already wet. My sleeping bag was wet. My sleeping pad was wet. But the wetness felt mild, and actually quite cozy. In January, I had been frozen stiff by this time of day; I had heard the ice cracking down on the pond and darkness had already fallen. Now it was sixty degrees out, even if the sun was barely visible.

I stayed under the tarp until eight. Then I grabbed my fly-fishing rod and walked down to the water. I cast out along the edge of the bog, trying every fly that I'd brought. At first I tried some artificial imitations of insects that might conceivably be hatching now and thus might possibly be a tempting menu item for a trout. Midges and the *Leptophlebia marginata* species of mayfly. After that I tried a few so-called attractor flies—big, bristly things that aren't necessarily a typical snack at this time of year but that might work to stir interest or aggression. I circled the entire pond. But not a single fish revealed itself.

It began to get dark and soon the rain started in again. My clothes had been damp for several hours and I began to feel myself getting cold. My orange Gore-Tex jacket no longer kept out the moisture. It was an expensive, high-quality jacket. The product label had said it was particularly beloved by alpine guides, and maybe this was the claim that had lured me to purchase it. I always fall for tricks like that. Perhaps the jacket was great in the Alps, but it was useless in the Norwegian woods.

The rain went straight through the fabric, and my shoulders were especially soaked. I know that managing moisture in wet conditions is one of the greatest obstacles for manufacturers of waterproof-breathable materials, because the outer fabric not only gets worn from wearing a backpack but the jacket is also tight against the skin at the shoulders, making it much harder to vent and keep the water out there. Nonetheless, I felt that such an expensive jacket should have done a better job. I cursed my own tendency to be taken in by advertising claims and sloshed across the bog and back to my tarp.

Everything under the tarp was sopping wet. I crawled in on top of my sleeping pad and lay in the pitch dark for hours listening to the rain. It would be a lie to claim that anything about the experience was comfortable; still, it was a nice change from my job and all of the end-of-year social events.

At one a.m., I decided to start planning my return. I needed to be in the city that morning for a meeting. I had seven hours before it would start. It would take me a few hours to walk home, and since I smelled pretty bad, I had to build in time for a shower. As well as to hang up my gear and clothes to dry. And to check my email to find out where the meeting would be. Maybe even prepare for it. If I was lucky,

I could accomplish all of this and still get four hours of sleep, which, I thought, isn't half bad for a Japanese salaryman.

It rained the entire way back through the woods. I was so wet there was nothing to lose. This thought in itself was liberating. Here walks a man who is wet to the bone, so you can just keep on falling, rain, it doesn't matter anymore! At my regular lunchtime spot, I stopped and peeled off my Gore-Tex jacket, rain pants, and underwear. They were cotton and soaking wet. I was now only wearing my wool socks, wool pullover, and wool long johns. All of these were wet through as well, but they kept me warm. I continued down the endless logging road and thought of Freud and Fugelli.

I scarcely have a death drive to speak of, and I rarely display any degree of aggression greater than my occasional Jan Baalsrud argument. And even though I enjoy walking alone in the woods at night wearing nothing but thin wool undergarments, that doesn't necessarily mean I'm an entirely antisocial being. I can enjoy social gatherings too. The challenge, in May, is to strike the right balance.

Walking along that logging road on a Thursday in January, with a heavy backpack on my shoulders and my winter boots creaking, Fugelli's phrase was on everyone's lips and I'd felt I had to ask myself the uncomfortable question: Who, exactly, comprises my flock? The answer was surprisingly easy. My flock is Trude and the kids, only these three. I spend 90 percent of my time with them, and of the remaining 10 percent,

I would prefer to spend as much of it as possible in the woods. Maybe others out there are like me, or maybe I am simply out of step with the times. In any case, I wish to round off this leg of my micro-expedition with a quote from someone I once knew who ended almost every sentence with the following words: *People are, when all is said and done, often very different.*

# JUNE

"Nature does nothing without purpose."

**ARISTOTLE**

NATURE'S WILD DIVE escalated. Everything sped up. June came. The shift to a new season was complete. Nothing was new anymore, and winter was a distant memory. The days rolled into one another. Soon it would be June 21, the longest day of the year and one of the most significant annual tipping points. Nature is full of such tipping points; each day, every hour something unexpected happens. But only two primary tipping points are fixed from year to year, for that is the way of nature's elementary logic: it gets lighter until it gets darker. It gets warmer until it gets colder.

The uncertainty that had characterized May carried over into June. Every day at least five changes in weather, each of them lasting for no more than an hour at a time.

My calendar of cultural obligations began to slacken. There were no longer as many events and celebrations. People, it seemed, had finally had their fill of hot dogs and ice cream and white wine in plastic cups. Perhaps now they were long-ing for vacation, for peace and quiet, for a few weeks free from the company of others.

June started off with the same mild temperatures as the sec-ond half of May. The weather was beautiful and everything grew greener and greener. Then came the rain. Torrential downpours accelerated the snowmelt in the mountains, resulting in flooding across several regions of Norway. This is an example of the inertia in the system that meteorologists are always talking about, I thought, scanning the online newspapers from my home office. When summer finally arrives, the last remnants of winter sneak through the back door disguised as frigid, murky floodwaters swelling through the valleys and ground-level apartments, and across culti-vated fields and farms and parking lots on the way to the sea.

It was early morning on the longest day of the year. As with my April excursion, this time I also planned to visit a differ-ent location than the little pond. And, as back then, this time the reason was also that I was going in search of something that couldn't be found at my regular campsite. This time, however, I felt certain I would be more successful than I had been on my search for grouse in April. Forgotten were the discomforts I had experienced in May. Also forgotten were

Freud's theories of aggression and the individual's conflict with civilization. The only feeling I now had was of expectation for what was to come.

I drove north with my two friends Geir and David. We are fly-fishermen. June is our month. All of the most significant events in a fly-fisher's life take place during a few short weeks in June, and the most important reason for this, besides the trout, has to do with that mythical creature, the mayfly.

We took two cars, Geir and David up ahead in the first one and I was behind them in my own. They were both going to return that evening while I, of course, planned to spend the night outside. Geir knew of a place that supposedly boasted promising numbers of the largest of all the mayflies, the *Ephemera vulgata*. The second half of June is when the vulgata undergoes its final metamorphosis into an insect that ventures onto land for a brief period before it dies. The larvae, or nymphs as they are called, rise to the surface of the water and the mature insects crawl out and up onto land. They can be up to about an inch long and look like little sailboats as they bob there, drying their wings on the surface of the water before lifting and flying off toward the shore. The *Ephemera vulgata* mayfly is such an enormous meal, a huge supply of protein, that it's hard to imagine a trout doing anything other than gobbling it up at the first opportunity. Such were my thoughts as I drove north in my car. The premise of this fishing trip was simple: if the vulgata were hatching today, the largest trout in the lake would be there.

We passed the suburbs that flank the north edges of the city. The sweeping residential area was barely visible through the thick foliage of blooming trees. The day was mild and overcast and there was hardly any wind. Farther north, a thick fog hugged the hillsides. A light drizzle covered my windshield. I put on country music and felt my anticipation rising. Mild temperatures, light rain. It was the kind of weather that made me think of the proverbial fish being shot in a barrel.

"The fate of our times is characterized by rationalization and intellectualization and, above all, by the 'disenchantment of the world,'" the German sociologist Max Weber claimed in his lecture "Science as Vocation." I find I have the same reaction to the expression "disenchantment of the world" as I do to Freud's "civilization and its discontents," which held so much meaning for me in May. I only vaguely recall what it actually means, but I often think about it and perhaps infuse it with my own substance.

As far as I can remember, Weber is claiming that an important dimension of meaning for the lives of humans was lost with the Scientific Revolution. For example, whenever an incomprehensible natural phenomenon took place in the past, people were compelled to devise their own explanations of it. They created stories and myths about such phenomena, and these stories often had a normative effect on peoples' lives. A thunderstorm or volcanic eruption, or even a flood, might have been interpreted as the wrath of the gods, and humans were forced to reflect: What have we done to stir up such anger? Is this horror deserved? And what can we do to avoid it in the future?

The Scientific Revolution ushered in explanations for these phenomena: electrical discharges in the atmosphere. Outbreaks of molten rock from the earth's interior, caused by high pressure. Glacial snowmelt coinciding with low-pressure systems and subsequent deluges.

Whereas the world had previously seemed mystical, almost magical, following the Scientific Revolution it was utterly trivial. Underlying meaning was reduced to dry, empirical facts. Whereas people had previously lived in subordination to so-called outside forces (God, the cosmos, nature), humankind now stood at the pinnacle of creation. The scientific and industrial and technological revolutions thus laid the foundation for the great exploitation of nature, which has continued until today. Suddenly, humans not only had the knowledge and the means to subdue nature and manipulate it according to their will—we also had the arrogance to do so.

The rest is history. Natural phenomena were analyzed and explained down to the minutest detail. The old tales unraveled. The world became disenchanted, and a fundamental dimension of meaning in the lives of humans was lost forever. According to Weber. And to me. Though in slightly different ways.

The lake Geir knew about was a big secret. The vulgata mayfly requires specific environmental conditions to thrive. Which is why you don't see them everywhere. But it does happen to thrive at this particular lake that Geir supposedly knew of, and this was not the kind of knowledge that he was about to divulge to just anybody. His definition of a flock to which one should tend is, if possible, even narrower than mine, and certainly light-years away from Fugelli's.

We arrived at the southern end of the lake. A light breeze blew in from the north, which made this the perfect place to start. The newly hatched mayflies weighed less than an ounce, and if the wind caught them up, those that didn't simply fly off would land again in the inlets and coves at the far end of the lake. We were well aware of this. As were the trout.

We crossed an old dike and a bright, barren pineland. We scouted out a headland consisting of a mountain and a relatively flat area with the occasional lanky pine tree. At the west end of the headland was a large green inlet. The terrain on the eastern edge was hillier. There was a floating peat bog there and across from it, tiny inlets with tall green grass protruding from the water. Some fallen old trees. Here and there, scattered water lilies.

We put down our packs and began assembling our equipment, all the while keeping watch across the water. There is no other situation in life in which I feel more at home than this. The start of a fishing trip. Ample time. Strong faith. No rush. Anything can happen.

We knew it was the right time of year, the right time of day, optimal weather. All of the pieces were in place, and this is rare, because if you are a fisher who fishes with dry flies, you know how rare it is that all the right conditions converge at the same time. We assembled our rods and reels, each attaching our own vulgata imitations at the end of the leader, and then we sat, waiting. An artificial fly is an exact replica of the real insect, and since the mayfly spends its final stage before dying drifting about the surface of the water, one must fish with floating imitations of the real fly. This is what's known as dry fly-fishing. It is a method in which you cast only toward rising fish, or toward fish that show themselves in some way at the surface of the water. If they don't rise, you don't cast. Countless fishing trips fit the profile of this latter category.

Mayflies are ancient, primitive insects comprising over three thousand different species spread across most regions of the world. In Norway alone there are just under fifty registered species. Even the name, mayfly, as well as its Latin name, *ephemerid*, alludes to the brief (and ephemeral) life span of this particular insect. In Norwegian, the mayfly is called a dayfly (*døgnflue*), though they live for more than a day. The English name, mayfly, is equally confusing because they do not live only during the month of May. This fact is apparent when observing these insects living out their final stages atop a forest lake in Norway in June. What we are witnessing as they skip across the water with their grand transparent wings is their fulfillment—their last brief hurrah—as they lay their eggs. Thereafter, they may die secure in the knowledge that they have completed their life's purpose.

The last stage in a mayfly's life is called imago. Before reaching this stage, they have lived hidden from the human gaze, far below the water, as small, oblong, and wingless nymphs no larger than an ant. The nymphs rise to just below the surface of the water and hatch, and the mature insects then emerge from their nymph shell and break through the surface of the water into the air. They drift for as long as possible on the surface, airing out their wings and—one might imagine—acclimating to these latest strange conditions of life.

At some point or other, the mayflies then alight from the water and head inland. But before they do, they provide the tastiest possible meals for trout. If you ever notice a fish jumping in June, chances are high that it's a trout that's just snatched a mayfly. Of course, other insects float on top of the water in the summer months as well. Some are there because their life cycle is not unlike the mayfly's (caddisflies, stone flies, midges); others are there simply because they decide to pause on the water during their flight to somewhere else (wasps, crane flies, St. Mark's fly, flying ants, moths).

However, the mayfly is widespread and exists in such large numbers that it makes up the bulk of a trout's summer diet. In fact, it is unlikely that trout would exist without the mayfly. These insects made the sport of fly-fishing possible for the British fishers of the mid-1800s who fished with split cane rods fashioned from triangular bamboo strips glued together and with silk lines that had to be impregnated with lard in order to float. In those days, flies were tied with natural materials, primarily fibers from bird feathers. Due to its many colonies, the British Empire had access to countless varieties of feathers from the far reaches of the globe, which of course influenced the overall appearance of the artificial flies.

The English also practiced releasing trout for sport into waterways, and these fish have since come to populate rivers far and wide. The result is that trout is now one of the world's most widespread fish species. The British have never been shy about doing whatever they please in the world and imposing their own unique traditions on their surroundings.

We sat on the headland staring into the water. After ten minutes, the first mayfly surfaced. At first there was nothing and then all of a sudden there was a vulgata sitting there. The creature was plump and magnificent, almost so large as to be frightening, and when you've seen a vulgata for the first time after a long winter, you always realize you'd forgotten how big it actually is. It simply appeared quite suddenly, as if it had materialized from thin air.

No one spoke. We kept staring. Here was another mayfly. Then two more. Five. Fifteen. Suddenly there were mayflies covering the surface of the water in the inlet, but we had yet to see any trout. This was not unusual. Maybe it isn't always like this, but it often takes a bit of time from when the mayflies hatch to when the trout start feeding. They have to notice the insects, of course, but just as important is that the trout first have to get it into their tiny little brains that these insects are, in fact, food.

The brain of a trout is about the size of a pea, and as such it isn't likely that trout have particularly well-developed memory archives from previous years. On the contrary, it almost seems as if they've forgotten everything, or else that for the sake of capacity, they stuff any remembrance of useful experiences down into the darkest corners of their minds. When something new happens, something which has happened to the trout in the past, they have to rummage around to retrieve this important information—and that can take quite a while. I like to think of a trout's memory as a room so tiny there's only space for one single thought at a time. If the mayfly comes in, the flying ant has to go out. If the midge comes in, the caddisfly is forced to leave. I don't know if that's truly how it works, but there's a certain sense to thinking like that, and it corresponds quite accurately to the reality one experiences during mayfly-hatching season.

For a trout to get it into its head that a vulgata—which, for all we know, it hasn't seen since last summer—is a nutritious meal, a whole host of mayflies must first float on top of the water. The sheer number of mayflies eventually stirs the far reaches of the trout's reptilian brain, *aha, that's food!* Once this message has been received, there's no turning back. From a different angle: this is also the moment when the trout forgets that everything *else* it likes to eat is also food—all of those other tasty morsels are forced out of the tiny space of the trout's brain—and what happens then is known in fly-fishing as selectivity. If a large number of a certain insect is at a particular stage of hatching, the trout can become so single-minded and focused on this insect alone that it rejects any other sources of food. If it happens to be in a phase of preferring to eat midge larvae, it might ignore a fat, juicy earthworm, even if the fisher is dangling the worm only half an inch from the trout's nose. The reason is that, in that exact moment and place, the earthworm ceases to become edible for the trout. Numbers are everything. Whatever insect happens to be out in droves is the trout's definition of food. This is basically the equivalent of spreading Nutella thickly on twenty slices of bread every morning before your kids finally realize that you've made breakfast and dig in.

The old English artificial flies were sometimes so colorful as to be downright tacky. The salmon flies in particular. The artificial mayfly flies, by contrast, look incredibly genuine even today and have been given poetic names: Pale Morning Dun, Blue Dun, and Greenwell's Glory. They resemble their natural prototypes, and so it seems natural to think they must have been made as pure imitations to lure the trout that swam in the English limestone rivers, those spring-fed, usually cold watercourses that wander gently through the gradually sloping countryside.

And yet, the advent of technical, modern, imitation fishing didn't really start until the 1980s. Up until that point in history, most artificial flies were fashioned out of pure fantasy, even if they still managed to deceive the gullible trout. Trout, after all, are not in possession of very sophisticated apparatus by which to distinguish the real stuff from the fake. But with the advent of modern imitation flies, precision became an important fly-fishing concept. A fly-fisher no longer cast a line at random and with an arbitrary fly on the end of the hook. Instead, the water temperature had to be measured, the contents of a fish's stomach examined, and imitations made of the genuine insects in their various stages of development. In this way, the fly-fisher imagined it was possible to understand nature down to the last tiny detail, to trick wild nature by its own terms, and to eliminate chances of failure. Fly-fishing became an empirical activity in which following a set of precise preparations should lead to a scientifically accurate outcome. This historical development smells a lot like Max Weber, but fortunately there is a limit to human scientific competence. There are many unknowns yet beneath the surface of the water that are impossible for fly-fishers to predict and therefore to take into consideration.

Time passed slowly out on the headland at the south end of the lake. Even a fly-fisher cannot remain eternally vigilant for mayflies hatching on the water. Concentration is exhausting. It is a state of mind which, by definition, is fleeting. It takes a lot out of a person to sit like that, staring alertly across the water without a single other thought in your brain.

The vulgatas continued to hatch, but still there weren't any trout rising to snap at them. We were flummoxed and thought perhaps the fish were simply late for their meal, that maybe it was like the Nutella metaphor and the number of mayflies would have to reach a certain magical number before the trout made their move.

Geir returned to the headland after several hours of fishing out on his secret peat bog somewhere. He reported that he had sat waiting quietly, as he is wont to do, and from what I know of my friend he would have been content to sit on the peat bog until next year's mayflies hatched. We didn't ask whether he'd caught anything. Nothing indicated that he had, nor did he volunteer a story. We meandered back and forth along the headland. David began boiling coffee on one of those modern rapid-boil propane burners and the water got hot in about one minute, which is three times faster than it takes on my more traditional Primus stove.

Here and there another mayfly continued to hatch. They would drift along on the surface of the water for several minutes before taking off, and none of them was getting eaten. We all agreed that we'd never experienced anything like this before, and that it was a clear violation—from nature's side—of natural rules and regulations.

After a time, a few caddisflies surfaced on the water. The caddisfly also hatches on top of the water, but after that, its life takes a very different turn from that of the mayfly. Whereas the mayfly floats like a graceful sailboat on the water's surface, the caddisfly drones about like a small, compact motorboat. There is something altogether dogged and working-class about it compared to the mayfly; they seem to be as different as the elves and dwarves in *The Lord of the Rings*.

Once the caddisfly emerges from its larval shell, it sets off at breakneck speed, seemingly without a thought for direction since only a matter of seconds ago did it undergo a radical physical transformation—and how in the world can an insect reflect on what to do next in such a short span of time? Caddisflies are large and clumsy; they leave waves and chaos in their wake as they veer toward land, their instincts undoubtedly warning them to hide as quickly as possible among the reeds and grass and stones—their instinct roars this at them until it goes hoarse—but not all of them succeed. I sat observing the caddisflies and considered that even nature has its defects. Not everything works the way it is supposed to, or perhaps this is also part of the plan; for example, that a certain number of caddisflies are supposed to end up as trout food.

Some of the caddisflies headed straight out across the lake. They continued in that direction for quite a long time until they realized it was the wrong way and then adjusted their course. We sat on the headland, following their wild route across the gleaming water. The water was barely more than a few yards deep in the middle of the lake, and under normal circumstances the caddisflies would have been in acute danger at that point. Their mad dash would usually have been like jumping out of the trench during the First World War and making a run for it across the frozen plains of Central Europe, but fortunately for them, that's not how it was on this day. On this day, there was a ceasefire. Every one of them made it to land. The caddisflies had no way of knowing it themselves, but they had chosen to hatch at the most opportune moment.

None of us could fathom what the trout could possibly be doing down there in the lake, but whatever it was, it must have been important. Why else would they allow such a feast to pass without partaking? Not a single caddisfly was made into fish food. They buzzed around in the slanted afternoon rays of light, and after a while we lost interest and left them to their own devices.

I sat alone at the tip of the headland. Geir and David were making dinner a bit farther inland. Just as I was about to stand up to stretch my legs, I noticed a very slight ripple in the water beneath a birch tree that inclined out over the lake. Though I hadn't seen what kind of insect the fish had taken, I knew it could not have been a caddisfly since the rise had been so cautious. On the end of my line was a vulgata imitation. I cast out. The fly came down lightly on the water just where the fish had stirred the surface. Then it dropped beneath the water. It was being pulled downward, cautiously, but without a doubt. There was no splash, no commotion.

Anyone who has ever fished for trout with a dry fly knows that the visual dimension is what makes this pastime such a unique—but sometimes also frustrating—experience. When you fish with an underwater line, you can't see the fish taking the fly or bait or worm. You only realize it once the fish is hooked. When you are fishing with a dry fly, by contrast, you see the fish take it immediately; however, if you are too quick to strike, you risk yanking the fly out of the fish's mouth. This is a great cause of worry for every dry fly-fisher, since one's instinct is to lift the rod immediately after seeing the rise. Overcoming the body's reflexes in this way and in such a situation is no easy task.

This time, at least, it went well, and maybe that had to do with the fact that I'd already been sitting there for hours without any kind of activity. I was sluggish, just sluggish enough, and the fish got hooked. I was focused on trout; I hadn't considered the possibility that it might be some other kind of fish, but the creature began to struggle in the water and I soon saw that it was in fact a small perch. It had a silvery gray belly and dark gray lines along its sides. A hint of green ran down its spine, and there were the characteristic red-or-ange pelvic and anal fins. I lifted it out of the water and broke its neck. This fish would be my dinner. I placed it down in the moss, and on my fingertips I could smell the unmistakable scent of perch caught in cold, fresh spring water.

When I was young, this day—summer solstice—signified that there were only two more days until the very best day of the year. My grandmother and grandfather lived next to a big lake that was brimming with perch, and according to the traditions in those parts, the perch pike could be caught with worms and floats starting on Midsummer Eve and onward, but never before. My grandfather was a farmer. In the summertime, he worked the fields. In the winters, he felled trees in the woods and dragged them out with a horse. He was, as I remember him, a mild, industrious man, and whenever he had time off from his work—the kind of time that philosopher Arne Næss calls "disposable" or "surplus time," what we might now refer to as "leisure"—he went to the woods. Not infrequently to fish.

My grandfather had two rules when it came to perch. Rule number one: Rod fishing with worms is not permitted before Midsummer Eve. Rule number two: Fishing is always best when it's raining. When it rained, he always had faith, he said. And so it was, though I never understood the correlation between perch, Midsummer Eve, rainy weather, and my grandfather's faith.

A lot of people think it rains too much in Norway in the summer, and maybe it does. But if you are a little boy whose only thought is of perch, and if your grandfather tells you that perch bite best when it rains, you might feel like it doesn't rain nearly enough in the summer in Norway. You might ask and prod every evening, "What will the weather be like tomorrow? Will it rain? Will it rain?" You don't want the kind of rain with storms and blustery winds, but you are eager for the kind of warm summer rain that falls quietly from the sky, meeting the surface of the water in a thousand tiny hushed pricks, so that in the end you can't tell where the water stops and the sky begins.

You will wait for this rain, and you will soon discover that it occurs as rarely as perfectly sunny days. And, when such a day comes at last, you know you'll have to take advantage of it. My grandfather knew this too. On days like this, he would let his work be, go out and dig up worms from behind the barn, and row out onto the lake.

We would sit there, he and I, in the skiff that my great-grandfather had built with his own hands. My grandfather was at the oars and I sat in the back. "See now," my grand-father would say, "now I have faith." I nodded and could feel myself filled up with a strong sense of happiness and what I think was certainty. I *knew* that the perch would bite on a rainy day such as this one, there could be no doubt. We looked at each other. Then we turned our attention to the white and red floats that bobbed on the slate-colored surface of the water. I cannot remember a single time when we ever returned empty-handed.

For me, perch fishing was an adventure. For my grand-father, it was another harvest. The fish that lived in the lake were a valuable supplement to the farm's food production, especially during the war years. In those days, my grand-father had enlisted as a young soldier. Even though the war was long since over by the time we went fishing together,

he remembered it with as much clarity as all the other vet-
erans who had served. He continued to fish the perch with
worms and floats in his "surplus time," and when he brought
them home, my grandmother would painstakingly rinse
and fry them.

The years passed. The two rules remained. But I could
not bring myself to accept my grandfather's strong faith
in tradition. I didn't have it in me, brought up as I'd been in
the 1970s to question these adopted truths. I knew by now
that Midsummer Eve was associated with the celebration
of the birth of Saint John the Baptist, and I would think to
myself: How can it be that perch adapt their food intake
to coincide with a Catholic holiday? What on earth does a
fish care about a world religion?

One year when the spring came, I challenged my grandfather. I suggested we should start fishing earlier to ease
the anticipation of waiting until later in the season. But, as
I recall, he was not very interested. He wasn't about to tam-
per with traditions; they had been handed down from my
great-grandfather, who'd had them handed down from my
great-great-grandfather. Perhaps he didn't even consider
these rules traditions, but the only true way to go about it.

I couldn't shake the thought that something about these
rules didn't add up. I was old enough to fish alone by this
time; I no longer needed to have an adult accompany me
in the boat. I went and got my fishing rod and a box of
worms. It was a day in June with a sharp wind and blue
sky. This was not the kind of day that would have given

my grandfather faith, even if it had fallen on the right side of the Catholic holiday, which it did not. But I didn't care about the weather or the date. I thought: Why does everyone in this village insist that the perch won't bite until after Mid-summer Eve? Have they ever even tried fishing earlier?

I rowed out to a place I knew to be a good spot. An hour later, the tradition had been invalidated. A handful of small perch wriggled at the base of the skiff and the distinctive odor of this fish when it's been pulled up out of the cold, early summer water pinched my nose. This was the same smell that now coated the tips of my fingers where I sat out on the headland of a lake in the Nordmarka forest several decades later, and I am certain that I would be able to identify this smell at any time, anywhere in the world.

The tradition solidly debunked, I rowed back, pulled the skiff onto the bank, and made sure to tie it up properly. I strung up the perch on a V-shaped rowan switch as I'd been taught and sauntered up to the farm while pondering how best to explain my catch. My grandfather was no longer a farmer by then. He had leased the land and taken a job at a factory in the city. He therefore was not at home when I reached the farm, and my grandmother told me he had just called to say he would be working overtime that day. She didn't seem bothered by the fact that the fish had been caught before Midsummer Eve—or else she saw how happy I was and decided not to show her displeasure. We rinsed the perch together. First, we cut off the heads. Then we cut each one along the spine from the tail fin to the neck. After that we took hold of the skin at the corner where the head had been and pulled it off in one decisive motion. Finally, we sliced off the tail fin and scraped out what little there was of entrails. When all of the perch had been cleaned, we wrapped them in plastic and put them in the freezer. I can no longer recall if I told my grandfather about my catch right when he got home or whether my grandmother let the fish stay in the freezer for a few weeks until a date safely beyond Midsummer Eve when they could join the other, properly caught perch and thus blend into the crowd.

It was late afternoon at the lake in the woods. I stood up, my joints stiff, and walked over to the others. None of us now believed the trout were going to rise on this day. Instead, we lounged idly on the slope. We lay on our backs and gazed up at the tree canopy. I thought about perch. I thought about Gunnar Larsen, the legendary news editor at the *Dagbladet* newspaper, who also wrote very good books. Larsen has said that he got the idea for one of his books while cleaning a perch net. When he first started cleaning the net, he didn't have a single thought in his head. By the time he was finished, the entire plot of his novel had been hatched, worked out, cut and dried. The only thing left was to start writing.

Geir and David gathered their things. The acknowledgment that this would not be a successful trout-fishing day had been lingering in the air for quite some time, and now they had decided to head home. They hoisted their backpacks, said goodbye, and then they were off, disappearing through the pine barren.

A calm settled over the water and the forest on this, the lightest day of the year. I stayed on the headland with a growing feeling of melancholy and senselessness, the way one always feels when one is alone in the woods. Only this time it was worse, since I had just been with other people. Talking was no longer a necessity, and when you are no longer talking, your attention naturally turns to your surroundings. The day grew slowly darker; the light petered out. Although things around me were still visible, they were grainier, like an old photograph.

I sat on a smooth piece of bedrock that sloped down toward the water. Gray rock, green moss, black leaves. The trees reflected in the water's surface. The sun had long since set. It was nighttime, but the sky was still illuminated. There was a stirring in an inlet on the opposite side of the lake. There is always something stirring on the opposite side of the lake.

I pitched my tarp beside a small rock face along the shoreline. Just as I had in May, I constructed an A-frame shelter with a three-foot stick at one end and a stick half that length at the other. I unrolled my sleeping pad and sleeping bag and collected my things. Filled my little pot with water for coffee the next morning. Tidied my fishing gear, took apart my rod, put the flies back into the tackle box. The artificial vulgata flies had been used for the first and final time that year. The mayflies had emerged as duns maybe only one week prior, and they would probably only remain in that stage for one week more before their molt to egg-laying spinners was complete and they'd fall spent to the surface of the water. This was my one chance to see this year's generation of *Ephemera vulgata*. When I returned to the woods in July, they would all be dead.

I ate crispbread and tubed cheese and drank bog water for dinner. The crunching from my teeth was loud in the quiet midsummer evening. If wood nymphs actually existed, they would certainly have heard it. And water sprites too, if they existed. A fog formed on top of the water; it was gray-ish-white and mystical against the floating peat bog. The fog indicated that the water was warmer than the air. It was long past midnight—the clock inched closer to one a.m., the darkest moment of the lightest day of the year, and yet it wasn't dark at all. Nonetheless, there was a troll-like atmosphere that got me to thinking that maybe wood nymphs and water sprites do exist after all.

I crawled into my sleeping bag beneath the tarp and thought again of Max Weber, and how the German sociologist probably hadn't taken into account that in spite of all our scientific explanations and crumbs of knowledge, it only takes a single, solitary summer night next to a woodland pond for the world to feel magical once again. This is what is often talked about as the "reenchantment of the world," and it is striking just how little it takes to enter into a completely different state of mind than our usual, modern, critical-rational state. From where I lay beneath the tarp, gazing out across the lake, scientific explanations were utterly useless. If a water sprite were to poke its head up from the bog, wet and looming and drippy, it would not have seemed the tiniest bit out of place.

I woke up at four. Or, I had already been woken up at two o'clock by a strange, protracted bird call. It was a sorrowful wail—*ouuu, ouuu*—several times in a row. I lay quietly, listening to the wailing sound and peering out over the motionless lake, which was shining and mysterious and recumbent. I fell back asleep, but at four a.m. it was time to get up.

It was already light outside. A pair of chickadees with their young were chirping away on a pine tree next to my campsite. They were squatters. Out of sheer laziness, they had obviously taken over the nest of a bigger bird since the entry hole was much too large for them. I had observed them the previous day too. Flitting back and forth to the nest, out and in, out and in, grasping insects, larvae, worms, and beetles in their beaks. They would land on a twig, twitch their heads side to side, keeping an eye out for danger, then dart into the hole, come back out again, and repeat the procedure. They didn't pause for a break until around ten in the evening. Then they stopped.

When I crawled out from under the tarp at quarter past four, these birds were already on the wing. They appeared at the hole of the nest, turning their heads side to side, looking for possible enemies, then they took off, and shortly after they returned with something delicious in their beaks.

I boiled water for coffee and sat watching the birds. They always have to be alert, these chickadees; they always have to fear the worst. The chickadees can never just kick back and forget about time and space, because if they do, there's a high likelihood they'll be eaten by something much larger than them. There are a lot of things bigger than a chickadee.

Death is ever present in the wild. The small are eaten by the big, and whatever is bigger than the big eats it too. This is how it goes for each and every forest inhabitant on its allotted level in the food chain. The evening before, I had noticed two beavers in a cove along the southeast side of the lake, and I was struck by the notion that these two munching machines appeared to be incredibly free from this endless cycle of multitasking to which the chickadees were bound. The beavers were hard at work, it was true, but they only had this single task and they didn't seem particularly worried about their surroundings. Maybe beavers don't have any natural predators within the eastern Norwegian forests, for what kind of creature would that be? What kind of creature in this forest would be prepared to catch and eat a beaver? None, I imagined, which is why a beaver does not seem to have a well-developed sense of danger. Instead it has been blessed with a sense of trust in its environment and a belief that it's possible to concentrate on the task at hand, to work in peace, and to complete the job that's begun free from the danger of interruption. It's the complete opposite for most other animals, including the chickadee.

I folded up my tarp, gathered my fishing gear, and pulled on my backpack. The lake was still, the mist hung thickly against the opposite shoreline. The sun began to peek over the ridgeline in the east. The first rays made the blades of grass on the swamp twinkle like diamonds. In that moment I found myself on the cusp of a tipping point. Starting today, nature would begin its shift in the only other direction it could possibly move. Every day would get a little bit darker, all the way until December 21, which would be my final night in the woods this year.

It's easy to feel a sense of melancholy on the lightest day of the year. It is easy to tend toward pessimism and negative thinking, but the way things work in nature is that the season we experience lags behind the astronomical season. Just like floods in June are caused by snow that accumulates in the mountains in winter, or the way the warmth of the sun in July or August follows weeks after summer solstice signals the arrival of summer. Water and mountains and land masses are warmed up and cooled down, warmed up and cooled down. It doesn't take a leap of imagination to understand that these processes take time.

By six a.m., I was back at my car and began the drive toward Oslo. My irritation from May had lifted like fog in the sunlight. I was nothing but harmony and joy. I'm half-way there, I thought contentedly as I bumped along the narrow logging road. Halfway there. My micro-expedition has gone well so far. And from here on out, it is only going to get darker.

The day after my return, I called up my friend Tarje, who has spent considerably more nights in the forest than I have. I told him about the strange, protracted bird call that had woken me up in the middle of the night. Tarje asked where I had been, and when I told him he was quiet. Then he finally said: "Do you know that there's a legend about that particular place?" "No," I said, "I didn't know about any legend." He told me that a young mother apparently once drowned her child in this lake, and people say she still walks about.

I thanked Tarje and told him I was glad that he hadn't mentioned this story until my return. I'm the kind of person who is easily spooked by stories like that, I explained. For example, I have deliberately never watched *The Blair Witch Project* because I'm worried that horror film might ruin a considerable portion of my life. That it could, in essence, force me to seek out other hobbies besides walking in the woods, other activities that take place exclusively indoors, in well-lit areas—like squash or Zumba or bingo or wine tasting. Tarje sniffed on the phone. "Not that I have anything against wine tasting," I added quickly, "but it's not really the same thing."

PART III

# SUMMER

# JULY

## A LIFE OUT OF DOORS

"In the forests and mountains, on the wide meadows
in the great solitude, one feels like a more natural, a
more wholesome person, one has the feeling that
there is something deeper which is one's true I, and
one returns with a fresher and healthier perspective
on the life that is lived out in cities. See, in the
wilderness, in the solitude of the woods, with a view
out over the vast meadows, is where the kind of
people are fashioned that our times sorely require."

**FRIDTJOF NANSEN,** *EVENTYRLYST*

M Y MICRO-EXPEDITION WAS halfway over. There
were six months behind me, six months ahead.
Ever since I first set out in January, I had often asked
myself the same question: What is it you are doing, exactly?
Going out to spend a single night alone in the woods each

month of the year, what's the point of that? Even now I have not managed to come up with a better answer than that I have always enjoyed being in the woods, and that I have always thought of it as an arena for recreation. The chance to breathe in fresh air, to move my body, to pay more attention to my surroundings than I tend to do, to fish, take pictures, build a fire, sleep outdoors. It's a cliché, of course. A big one. But that doesn't make it any less true.

A lot of people share my tendencies, and for most of us, July is the month when we finally set out to tackle the plans we dreamt up in the winter. The number of nights spent in a tent are statistically higher in July than in any other month of the year. Backpacks and mosquito spray and sleeping bags and sleeping pads and camp stoves and coffeepots and fishing rods—all of the gear we've been brought up to believe is essential to living a worthwhile life in this country.

Of course, it's not really accurate. This notion of what makes life worth living is the result of a particular historical tradition and a narrow view of nature. I have the greatest respect for people who choose to let the forest be the forest and live out their lives in the city instead. I don't hold the belief that people are happier or live better lives simply by spending time in the wild. Fridtjof Nansen thought so. Arne Næss too. But personally, I think it's going a little too far. The issue isn't about being a better or worse person or living a worthwhile or constrained life. Rather it's about how and where you thrive and what you enjoy doing. For some, that means going shopping in a global metropolis. For others, it means spending single nights alone in the woods. And for many people, it's both.

People who spend a lot of their free time in outdoor pursuits often let it be known that they consider these activities more valuable than other hobbies. They have an irritating tendency to want to impose their own preferences on others, both on individuals and families. In Norway, this tendency runs deep. This traditional view is in our bones, but it has a shorter history than one might think. The idea that all of one's free time should be spent in the outdoors hasn't always been the prevailing opinion. Even the Norwegian idea of *friluftsliv,* or "fresh air life," was invented at some point. A thousand years ago, or even only three hundred years ago, people lived in the wild. They were born and died there—they didn't know any other existence—and so it is quite unlikely they had a philosophy of spending time outside in contrast to their daily lives.

July is the month of the year when Norwegians tend to spend most of their time outside. The temperatures are warm, it is light almost around the clock, and many schools and businesses close for summer vacation. And though the evenings are starting to get darker and drawing closer to winter, this month marks the high point of Norwegian summer. It is in July that the vegetation blooms; it is in July that all of the elements reach their peak temperatures before

slowly cooling down again. The mountains and the water—
yes, even the earth is at its warmest.

My family was going to spend four weeks of summer
vacation at our cabin by the sea starting in July. It rained
every day up until the day of our departure. As we packed
the car and left, however, the sky turned clear and blue, and
that's how it remained until the end of our vacation. Thirty
days straight of sunshine and no wind. None of us could
remember another summer like that. We rambled about in
the coastal landscape: every day started without a plan, each
day simply came into being on its own, and each resembled
the ones before it so we could hardly tell them apart, these
days. Time seemed to stop, and our bodies and our minds
slipped into a rhythm that can only be the result of ample
time—ample time and the absence of commitments.

July was the complete opposite of May. There was no dis-
content due to matters of civilization; there were hardly any
matters of civilization to speak of. Mostly it was just the four
of us. We swam and fished and barbecued and went walking and rode around in our boat; we paddled our canoe and
made little excursions and invited friends over and ate ice
cream. One evening after the kids had gone to bed—naked
and suntanned on top of their blankets—I got out my computer and proceeded to look at photos from the winter part
of my micro-expedition. It was a strange experience. Hundreds of identical themes. Snow. Tracks through the snow.
Icicles. Snow-laden trees. Was I the one who had taken these

photos? I thought. Had I really been there? The themes felt unreal to me now. And yet, I felt a curious tugging sensation toward this landscape, the rawness of it, its dramatic, uncompromising nature.

By mid-July, the coastal landscape had already begun to shift. Whereas the vegetation had been a brilliant green color at the start of our vacation, it began to yellow. This transformation happens earlier where the smooth, gently sloping bedrock, called *svaberg* in Norwegian, dominates the landscape, where the soil is thin, where the terrain faces south. Of course, the rapid change in the color of the leaves had to do with the fact that there had been so little rain that summer, but also that summer had reached its zenith. There were still a few days before I would leave for the seventh stage of my micro-expedition, and I found myself thinking, as I meandered about, what the woods would look like now. Would they be different than in June? Would I find yellow, drying leaves there as well?

When at last I set off, it was late in the afternoon. I felt extraordinarily happy. A solitary overnight trip in July. A vacation within a vacation, privilege within privilege, joy in the midst of delight.

I was returning to my pond, only this time from a different approach. I had already spent time poring over my map and there were a handful of trails I could choose. On my way to the pond, I knew I would pass several other small bodies of water, among them some that are popular with families and berry-pickers, as well as your average backpacker.

I parked the car, grabbed my backpack, and started to walk. At first I walked along a gravel road hemmed in on every side by green, under canopies stretched widely overhead that cleansed the air and produced life-giving oxygen for all of earth's inhabitants. Beneath these large and cascading branches, full of birds and insects and thick with foliage, I walked on a moss-covered forest floor that plunged steeply down on the road's west side while on the east side a stream trickled. A small stream, after weeks without rain.

As I continued my walk into the woods, I thought about Peter Christen Asbjørnsen, the Norwegian collector of fairy tales like the brothers Grimm, who had spent so much time in this exact spot. In Asbjørnsen's day, which was the first half of the eighteenth century, back when "outdoor recreation" was not a phrase in the vocabulary, the lives of most people in Norway and around the world was closely linked to the outdoors, though not recreationally. A large portion of people's lives was spent outside, not inside. Among other reasons, therefore, it became common during this era to use the term "leisure" to refer to the time spent not working, otherwise known as "free time."

This idea of spending time outside during one's free time was imported to the countryside by tourists, usually from the upper class, often from England. Salmon fishers and mountain climbers in search of unadulterated nature who employed the locals in their pursuits. As mountain guides. Or to help them net their catch. The British travelogue *Three in Norway by Two of Them* by Walter J. Clutterbuck and James A. Lees provides a unique glimpse into this tradition, as well as a fascinating perspective on how the sophisticated, upper-class English authors viewed the much-less-sophisticated Norwegian locals.

Henrik Ibsen is considered one of the first Norwegians to use the term *friluftsliv*, a word in my language that implies healthy outdoor leisure activity, and that has become such a popular concept in Norway that it embodies an almost religious philosophy for healthy engagement in the outdoors. Ibsen's first use of the word occurred in the poem "On the Heights," which was published in 1859. The line reads: *friluftsliv for mine tanker,* or roughly "fresh air for my thoughts." In the earliest English translation of the poem, the idea was cut altogether for the sake of a flowery rhyming scheme; however, a later translation renders Ibsen's line as "time to think at leisure." Only nine years after Ibsen's poem, in 1868, the Norwegian Trekking Association was founded, and "outdoor recreation" as we know it today was thus established and organized in the second half of the 1800s. It was the Norwegian explorer Fridtjof Nansen, however, who best formulated this concept of *friluftsliv* and whose definition has become the cornerstone for the way Norwegians think about spending time outside and how this relates to ideas of naturalness, originality, health, and identity.

In spite of his softer edges, Nansen was also a classical, masculine explorer undertaking daring feats and clearly and elegantly articulating a philosophy of the world that has secured him an undisputed place in Norwegian history. But as I hiked in the direction of my pond, my mind was filled with thoughts about that other explorer, Asbjørnsen, who passed this way over 150 years ago and whose motive for walking in the woods was astonishingly similar to my own.

Although Asbjørnsen also holds a position of respect in Norwegian history, he is first and foremost known as a gatherer of folk stories. What many people don't know is that he was also one of the first Norwegian writers to formulate the thoughts that have since come to express the foundation for how we relate to and understand nature. He first expressed such thoughts in the tale "A Summer Night in a Norwegian Forest" and then again in "A Night in the Nordmark Forest," both of which are in the collection *Norwegian Fairytales and Folktales* that was co-authored by Asbjørnsen and Jørgen Moe in two volumes in 1845 and 1848, roughly ten years before Henrik Ibsen first coined the term *friluftsliv*. Asbjørnsen doesn't use the term in his writing; however, it is exactly the same concept he describes. "A Night in the Nordmark Forest" opens with these sentences:

*One day in July, as clear as a September day, a ray of sun coming over the hilltops, an arbitrary scent of spruce riding the air in the midst of the sweltering heat in this oppressive city stirred my wanderlust and all my longing for forests and open fields. There was*

> *nothing for it but that I simply must and would go out, to breathe*
> *in the fresh air of rivers and trees.*

Already in the first sentences it's possible to detect the kernel
of those values that many of us attach to the philosophy of
*friluftsliv*: free time, freedom, stillness, contemplation, a state
of being that is close to the original state from which we
came. There is an incredible syncretism between these
sentences and the later words of Nansen's more pro-
grammatic essays. One additional reason that I like this
particular tale by Asbjørnsen is that it not only touches
on ideas held by Nansen, but that it also follows a small
excursion. Asbjørnsen does not have much time for leisure. Thus, he sets off in his tale on a micro-expedition of
his own. It's important to remember that, in his era, there
was much more untouched wilderness between the main
street of Oslo—Karl Johans gate—and the heart of the
Nordmarka forest than there is in modern times. Sunday
hikers often turned back just outside of what now comprises
the center of downtown Oslo for fear of being attacked by
wild animals.

Asbjørnsen's path through the woods was not unlike my
own. He began down in Christiania, the former name for
Oslo, and must have hiked up past the stretch of villas where
I live and farther up until he reached the Maridalen valley
before venturing over the ridge with a glimpse of Skjærsjøen
lake glimmering between the pine trees below and then

following the Bjørnsjøelva river to Bjørnsjø lake and continuing on through the forest from there.

At this point, he crossed paths with two landsmen, the fisherman Elias and a man he referred to only as a Hadelander, or a man from Hadeland. It was dusk. Asbjørnsen sat around a fire telling stories with the Hadelander and Elias the fisherman—or more precisely, Elias told stories and the other two listened. The stories were about wood nymphs, treasures and treasure seekers, a vein of silver as thick as a tree trunk on the bottom of Blankvann lake. Others were about inexplicable blue lights in the woods at night, the pagan yule goats and bears and beasts of unimaginable proportions, and how the hobgoblin settled at Sandungen lake, "and many others who had come to live in the Nordmark forest in the old days." In spite of the superstition and dark portents of Elias's disturbing stories, a feeling of calm and harmony enveloped the trio as he spoke.

I had brought almost nothing along on my night out in July. I didn't have a knapsack as Asbjørnsen had, but I did bring a small daypack with the essentials in it, and after two weeks of chopping wood and wheelbarrowing and other physical activities at the cabin, my body felt light and strong. I decided to sprint for a short stretch, but I quickly tired of that and returned to my normal good sense.

The forest didn't seem to be exhibiting any of the signs of dryness that were present along the coast. Everything spoke of verdant freshness; everything smelled vibrant and clean.

Yet there was noticeably more of one element: wild grass. The grass had barely been visible when I'd been there in June, or maybe I hadn't noticed it because the blades were green like everything else around them. They had since turned a pale yellowish color that stood out from all the green. The tall stalks swayed in the soft afternoon breeze, filtering the slanted sunlight that settled on their heads, as if resting there.

I came to an open glen and sat down on a rock to eat and rest. As I sat, I heard for the first time that year the sound of grasshoppers singing. Perhaps there is a mysterious connection between the emergence of golden stalks of grass and grasshoppers singing, I don't know, but I cannot recall ever experiencing one without the other. Go ahead and try it: it's impossible to separate them. It's my impression that grasshoppers start to sing around the same time that the grass first begins to dry out and turn golden, and maybe there is a natural explanation. In any case, it is the sound of high summer, one of the first signs that this season will also eventually come to an end.

Every year, someone or other insists that they can no longer hear the singing of grasshoppers. The high-frequency noise is one of the first things to disappear from audible range as we age and our hearing grows weaker. I sat on the rock thinking of my grandmother. I remember she told me when she first realized this loss in her own hearing, and that was the first time I had ever considered that the way we experience nature is connected to whatever senses we have intact. "I can't hear the grasshoppers anymore," said my grandmother, and there was a wistfulness in her voice, as though she knew they were there even though she could no longer hear them, because nature had started to take on the hues that it gets when the grasshoppers start to sing. It's easy enough to notice something new when it is placed front and center, in the foreground of an old image. But it's not as easy to recognize when a single tiny detail that's always been present has vanished from the same image. My grandmother noticed. She stood on the terrace in the late summer evening, full of the realization that something was missing. Nature had been transformed into a film scene without its most important soundtrack. Over eighty years, her body had grown used to the fact that whenever the eyes see yellow stalks of grass and a red moon, the ears are supposed to take in the sound of grasshoppers. But they no longer did. The grasshoppers were there, but not for her—and this memory reminds me of an old ballad about time passing and everything, eventually, coming to an end.

I passed a large lake just as the sun was setting behind ridgetops in the west. This particular lake is a popular camping destination for forest-goers, and in July there are a lot of them. A couple with a noticeable age gap, or else a mother and her son, had set up their tent at the first obvious campsite. I walked in a large detour around their camp because I didn't feel like talking to anyone. The pair had a campfire going and they had stretched a clothesline between two trees.

The line was full of clothes, which made it seem like they'd been there for quite a long time, or else each of them required an enormous wardrobe. Maybe, I mused, they were newly in love in spite of their great age difference and so wanted to dress up for each other, even out in the middle of the wilderness, and thus they had to keep going back into the tent to change into new outfits.

I kept on along the eastern shore of the lake. I passed a family of three: a mother, father, and little girl. The girl toddled around the water's edge as her parents kept a close eye on her. They stood like herons, their upper bodies stiff and their eyes vigilant, because the water was dark and the bottom was soft and muddy, and I knew from my own experience what this was like. They had pitched their tent. It seemed they too would be spending the night.

Not much farther along, I passed a father with a small daughter about the same age as the other little girl, and they had pitched a tent as well. After that, I ran straight into four friends who were stretched out, lounging in the tall grass, each with a fishing pole by his side. I nodded hello to the four friends and continued out toward a peninsula.

At the tip of the peninsula, I found a headland where the bedrock, warm from the sunlight, slanted down into the deep, blue water. I sat down without really knowing why. I had no real intention other than to sit in this spot for a while before continuing my trek around the lake and up toward my own little pond.

Throughout the day, the sky had been clear and there had been a soft sea breeze. The swallows flew high and a buzzard lamented from over the hill across the water.

Once the sun went down behind the western ridges, things grew quiet. It was the kind of evening when everything in nature is stable and predictable. The water was smooth as glass, the trees stood silently, the sky turned a deeper shade of blue in the east, and it was hard to imagine that nature could look any different than it did in that very moment.

But idylls are made to be broken. On the opposite shore, the father of the little three-person family began to scold his daughter. He wanted her to pose for a photo, but she wasn't listening. "Stand there! Yes, like that! Hold still! No, no, no!" the father screamed, apparently clueless to how well sound carries over the water. His voice grew shriller and more desperate. The daughter said nothing. The mother said nothing. Couldn't he just give up on his photography project? Didn't he know that kids never like to pose? Didn't he know that the only thing he could possibly end up with was a contrived scene with malcontented models?

The father's nagging continued, his intensity mounted. I was convinced this adventure must have been his idea. His daughter didn't harbor any notions of outdoor recreation, of course, and the mother had probably known that something like this was bound to happen. Maybe she was feeling dread right then; maybe she knew that because he felt he was finally in charge of their domestic situation, he was going to show them the harsh and merciless reality of the wilderness in an era mostly defined by diaper-changes and morning conversations with day care staff about food allergies and the consistency of one's child's poop.

I pictured the scene. Maybe they were starting to realize they'd bitten off more than they could chew, that overnight camping trips that involve sleeping in a tent never quite turn out the way you imagine they will when you are planning them from the comfort of your home. The situation felt very familiar. That father could easily have been me.

The little peace and quiet that was left on the headland was quickly shattered by a swarm of gnats that decided my head was the perfect gathering place for the evening. At first, I let them buzz around me, wishfully hoping that if I just ignored them they might go away. But gnats are gnats. They aren't small children or smartphone salespeople. A gnat never gives up. Each one of them sought out every opening in my head: my eyes, nose, ears. It took only seconds for them to find these spots, and they were so tiny that it was useless to defend myself, as I sometimes defend myself against mosquitoes—at least under normal circumstances. Whenever I stopped batting my hands for more than three seconds at a time to do something else, the gnats were everywhere. I knew they would let up once it got really dark, but I wasn't willing to wait that long.

I stood and put on my backpack and then resumed walking through the forest along a narrow path that led to the top of a ridge. It was noticeably darker than in June, but it was still light enough out that I didn't have to wear my headlamp. When I reached the saddle, I followed the ridgeline until I was at the same elevation as the little pond. I continued on through blueberry shrubs and over bogs. By the time I finally arrived, it was the darkest I expected this night in July would get. I lit a fire and set up my tarp, and when the embers had almost completely burned out, I tossed water over the rest of them and went to sleep.

I woke early as usual. The weather was the same: blue sky, no wind. But there was more moisture in the air now: the underside of the tarp was wet, and in the grass on the peat bogs, drops twinkled in the spiderwebs. I boiled water for coffee on my camp stove. Life was good. I didn't have to return to my home office that day. Instead, I would go back to the cabin by the sea, back to my vacation.

Asbjørnsen must have experienced something similar as he wandered through the Nordmarka forest; the tone of his stories suggests a person in his element. He doesn't offer exhaustive analysis about why he feels so at home in the woods; he simply explains that the city is clammy and oppressive and that the woods are the opposite. But still, between the lines, you can read what he is saying: ample time. Real people. There's nothing artificial about them: they are sober, down-to-earth folks, and they represent an ideal for cultivated elites from the city. Increasingly, there is a notion that something has been lost in civilization: that nature is pure and original while modern, polluted city life represents a kind of fall from grace. It is an idea that Nansen and many others developed, and that today constitutes the core of our ideas about *friluftsliv* and healthy, nature-integrated living.

Asbjørnsen's trek through the woods happened at a time when industrialization was taking off in Norway. And Asbjørnsen's adventures represent a re-mystification of the world; they reinfuse it with superstition—and perhaps thus with meaning. For Elias the fisherman, something is hidden behind every tree in the woods.

Several things characterize this story of Asbjørnsen's. One obvious trait is that it is distinctly romantic, as stories of that era often were. Asbjørnsen meets many colorful characters on his journey. All of them are introduced as sober wilderness people in possession of a type of knowledge or wisdom that city folks do not have. At no point does the text express dissatisfaction; there are no negative descriptions. Apart, that is, from the opening sentences in which all of the negativity describes the city. Asbjørnsen was a nature Romanticist; first and foremost, he saw what he wanted to see. There's another trait too that I've often noticed in "A Night in the Nordmark Forest." The version of the story that I have read, and which I believe is the original, is full of errors. It is so rambling and untidy, both in its punctuation and grammar, that it can be hard at times to get the gist of the story. I like to think the explanation is as follows: Asbjørnsen returned home from his journey through the woods and sat down to write in his garret in Christiania. He began to write down the story, maybe in a single sitting, realizing of course that there were a few mistakes, but then he was overtaken by the urge to travel and to go on another adventure and thought: Who cares about grammar! Other people can worry about that. As for me, I'm off to the woods once more to find another story!

That same afternoon, I found myself back at the cabin, picking up my family summer vacation exactly where I'd left off. Nothing had changed. It was as if I'd never even been away. Trude and the kids had barely taken note of my absence, I simply glided back into the same role as always and there I stayed.

The days passed, and I gradually transformed more and more into a cabin-dwelling person, the kind of person whose only worry in life is how the boat is moored. But I soon discovered a point on a mountain below the cabin where I could take a leak and check on the boat at the same time. It was a particular spot with an opening in the leaves that gave me the perfect line of sight out to the little dinghy with its outboard motor. And with that, I had now also eliminated this single problem of a cabin dweller.

Nothing unforeseen happened, except that the weather remained exceptionally fair. Our family is like other families. We bring a certain set of expectations with us to the cabin. The family has its collective set of expectations (shared meals, shared games, go for walks, sleep in), and each individual has their own personal set (build a patio, befriend a crab, create a vegetable garden, build a spaceship).

These expectations are laboriously built up over the long winter, but when they are finally confronted with the reality of summer vacation, they quickly dissipate. They are forgotten, or merely evaporate; it's as if the tempo at which things take place at the cabin does not allow for such ambitions, as if the atmosphere itself causes them to crumble to pieces. After only a few days, everyone pads around at their own tempo, no one can recall what it was they had thought about doing, and if anyone were to ask what they had been doing before they came, extra time would be needed to recall this information. This is the point during the vacation when all sense of time comes to a halt. If you try to remember your vacation once it's over, you will undoubtedly be able to recall the very first days with ease, these first days are framed by the concrete: arrival, unpacking, putting out the boat, the first barbecue, the first dip in the sea. But after that, it's hard to distinguish any one thing from any other.

If you really want to gain any sense of passing time, you must look to the natural world. When we first arrived, it was early July, almost pre-summer. Everything was green. Since then, the first blueberries had ripened, and after that the raspberries, and the mackerel had come closer to shore. Then we could see the gar—that slender silver fish that looks foreign and tropical—hunting herring down at the sea when it was quiet in the evenings, dashing back and forth, always on the move. Around the same period, the fledgling gulls left the reefs for the first time after birth and began swaying above the cabin, faltering at first and then eventually more steadily until they finally looked as if they had always hung suspended above us. There were flowers everywhere. The young swans still swam with their parents along the shore, but they got whiter and whiter and their parents were no longer quite so cautious about keeping them with the rest of the flock. Green grass in the bedrock fissures slowly turned yellow, so slowly that we hardly noticed it, until one day we suddenly saw that it was more yellow and red than green down near the water and we stared thoughtfully and wondered if so much time had indeed passed. Then came the characteristic orange of the rowan berries and the juniper berries, of which there are so many below the cabin. They sparkled like precious stones in the morning dew. Now it is late summer, we thought, and we felt the first wave of melancholy.

One of the last evenings before our vacation came to an end, I took a final hike to my boat-lookout point. It was ten o'clock, maybe ten thirty, maybe eleven, and the water was so still that the boat would have stayed in place even without the moorage lines. It was nearly dark out, and this darkness was of a different variety than when we'd first arrived. Not only did it get darker sooner, but the darkness was also thicker, less transparent. This was another sign of late summer, in the same way that yellowed stalks of grass and long shadows are too. And the grasshoppers that sing as if life were nearing its end, which in a way it probably is. I told myself what I'd told myself the previous year: you have to buy a book about grasshoppers, you have to learn why they start to sing at precisely this time of year, and you have to find out where they spend the first half of the summer. As I stood there peeing from my lookout point at the end of July, it seemed obvious that I needed to buy a book about grasshoppers, but the previous year it had felt that way too and yet I had never bought that book. As soon as I got home, I forgot all about the grasshoppers and didn't remember them again until the following year, which was now this year. The other insects suffer the same fate: I think of them only during the brief weeks when I see them. And here they were, pitching to and fro, confused and aimless, their movements signaling autumn. Foremost among these is the moth. It is drawn toward the light when it gets dark in the evening; it can't let the light alone. Something deeply anchored inside of it says *that's where you should fly, little moth,* over and over again. And in the morning the moth is too tired to do anything at all, so it just sits there, as if glued to the cabin siding, until late into the day it stretches its wings, takes off, and flutters into a thicket or into the grass.

There was also the full moon. The previous moon was yellower than the one that had come before it, and that thought was almost enough to make me start yearning for fall.

But before that, I wanted more summer. I wanted to stay longer, I wanted to visit the cabin again as soon as I could. So after we had packed the car and driven back to the city, after we had gone to pick up our mail and mowed the lawn and the kids had submerged themselves in all of the toys and games they had forgotten about, then I might say: "Damn, I forgot to bring up the boat."

# AUGUST

═══════

"I came here when I was very young. I came back many times. Most often in my thoughts. In times of conflict and strife. Or in the night, when I was unable to sleep. In those times, I imagined myself wandering on half-invisible paths, to hidden glades and quiet waters. Void of humans, but full of life, of birds and insects, the sound of summer forests: the buzzing of wasps and flies, great purple beetles, like soaring gemstones between the grayish-black pine branches, in across the fermenting bogs and sumps. And there would be old, graceful moose chewing in the dark thickets, and echoes of the wood grouse's clucking. Summer would turn to fall, with hoarfrost and ice on the withered willowherb. I could picture it all clearly. The snow that fell in here on an early, early winter morning. And the sound of the brooks in the spring. The grouses at play.

I lay there knowing that as soon as I was old enough, it was here I would come. Alone, never with anyone else."

INGVAR AMBJØRNSEN, NATTEN DRØMMER OM DAGEN
(THE NIGHT DREAMS OF THE DAY)

I AM OFTEN AMAZED at how little I am able to remember from my own life. It isn't that I have a problem reconstructing what I've done and where I was at a certain time: when I studied here or there, when I traveled, when I moved there, when I worked here. All of these experiences have been archived in my memory. It's just that astonishingly few of these are strong memories. They are not associated with any particular feelings or emotions. When I stop to consider most of my memories, they seem almost encyclopedic. They aren't recollections of concrete moments, the sensory kinds that can be remembered without words, or experiences that feel fresh and new with each recall.

A disappointingly large portion of my overall memory appears to be more like a tidy record of my life. However, every now and then there are moments, scenes that, when recalled, are as full of life as they were when I first experienced them. Maybe this is what memories are, and maybe the difference between memories and recollections is that memories mean something for the person who has them; they represent moments in the past that have had a particularly formative impact. We like to think—at least, I like to think—that such memories tell us something about who we are deep down and who we wish to be. Their most prominent trait is that they cannot simply be called to mind whenever we beckon them; rather, such memories surface when you least expect it. And for my part, they are—without exception—formed from a sensory experience related to nature.

The summer vacation was over. We had said goodbye to the smooth bedrock, the beach, the boat, and the seagulls. We were back in our four-person home, once again surrounded by the routines of everyday life. Whereas in July it had taken us a week to adapt to the slow rhythms of vacation time, it took us only a single day to return to our ordinary urban tempo. Work and day care, after-school programs, and leisure activities. New business meetings were scheduled, the new roster of parental volunteer duties at the co-op day care was drawn up, filling our hours. Our life's routine balance was restored and we shook off the melancholy of summer's end.

I would have liked our summer vacation to go on, but it was with renewed vigor that I began to plan my August trip to the woods because I could sense a change in the air. The evenings had become markedly darker. The darkness had another quality to it; it was thicker, no longer as transparent as it had been in the middle of summer. The moon was big and bright. The greens of early summer had been replaced with yellows and oranges and reds, and the damp freshness of nature through spring and summer had shifted to something more arid.

Over the course of the entire summer, my son had often piped up that he wanted to come with me to the woods. By then I'd been going out on my micro-expeditions since the new year, and of course he had noticed all my outdoor gear and listened to my stories about the moose and the foxes. He was four years old, and as with most four-year-olds, there was an enormous gap between his actual abilities and his belief about what he was capable of. His sense of his own bravery and courage was much grander than his actual bravery and courage. Up to that point, he had proven himself to be neither especially brave nor determined. Thus, I had deflected by gently telling him that the following year, when he turned five, he could come with me on an overnight camping trip.

It was a meaningless response to offer a four-year-old. Next year, for him, meant never. Next year might as well have been another lifetime completely unrelated to him; it was an excruciating abstraction. So, on the first weekend after the start of school, we sat down together to study the map.

It was early on a Saturday morning. The girls were still asleep. He said that he wanted to go to Bærum, a small county that he knew of because he has a friend who lives there. I told him that of course we could go to Bærum, but another time. "Today we are going to the Nordmarka forest, the woods that start at the lake where you sometimes go with your day care," I said.

I packed my big backpack and he packed his tiny one. We left a note on the kitchen counter so the girls wouldn't wonder where we'd gone. In fact, they already knew where we were going and how long we'd be away. But this little note made us feel bigger and more important; it gave us a very special feeling that we were embarking on an expedition early in the morning and we were leaving behind a little note with a reassuring and informative message for those who stayed behind at home.

We climbed into the car and drove out of the city. My son asked me from the back seat where we were going. I told him a bit about the spot, about the pond and the path there. When I looked into the rearview mirror, he had already fallen asleep.

Nearly all of my childhood memories stem from moments in the early morning or else late at night, and all of them involve a smell. It is the air I breathe in that infuses these memories with power, and nowadays whenever I inhale one of these scents, the associated memory pops up instantaneously and in shocking clarity. I am back where I once was, and suddenly I am taking everything in and feeling the same feelings that I felt back then. I use the word "feeling" because that's what it is, a feeling; it doesn't have anything to do with thoughts. It is a wordless feeling, but so brief, a puff of air, nothing more, and then it is gone. It is not the detailed recollection of all I've experienced, but the memory as a physical sensory experience. After that initial inhalation through my nose I may recognize the scent again with my next in-breath, but this time I am prepared. I have anticipated it and it doesn't seem nearly as powerful; I can't wrangle myself back to the same state because the memory doesn't surface on its own in the same bold way. This very fact suggests the unique power of memories: that you cannot actively retrieve or search for them; they come when they come, unintentionally and suddenly. And just as suddenly they are gone again.

After an hour of driving, we arrived. I parked along the side of the road and woke up my son in the back seat. He opened his eyes and peered around, confused. From his expression, I could see that he neither knew where we were nor why we were there. I explained that we had arrived, that we were going to camp outside for a night, and that our trip began there.

"Are we in Bærum?" he asked.

"No," I answered, "we are in the forest."

When we had sat down to look at the map at the break-fast table earlier that morning, I had come well prepared. I had already studied the area and chosen a suitable spot. I'm not the kind of person who believes it's important to push your children to their limits. I just don't have it in me. My children will thus probably come to resent this fact later in life when they realize they're not going to be professional soccer players or actors on the national stage. Aside from the Jan Baalsrud argument I often evoke at home, though only ever because we are in a rush and have to make it to school on time, I almost never push them to do anything. I am also not the kind of parent who insists that children are better people if they spend a lot of time outside. I tire of hearing people insist on this, or reading the endless stream of social media posts about the three-year-olds who hike for five miles without a single complaint. It just isn't true. The only truth one can glean from such a post is that this family has certain ideas about what a family should be, and that it is desperately trying to appear like their ideal. Healthy, hardy, and unified.

We are not that kind of family. Our collective abilities are limited to barbecuing at our cabin and swimming in the sea and picking berries somewhere close by. For this reason, I had chosen as our destination a lake that was just a short walk from the trailhead parking lot. One mile, maybe two tops, along relatively flat terrain. A trail, in other words, for a four-year-old whose short legs get tired before long and who is sometimes scared of dark woods and whose mood when that happens can quickly turn from lightness and joy to inconsolable tears and a stubborn refusal to keep walking, regardless of how far it might be back to the car.

We took one last look at the map. Then we put on our backpacks and started to walk.

"This is where our expedition starts," I said. "Are you ready?"

"I'm eddy," said my son.

August began the way July ended, which is to say warm and dry with colors that turned yellower by the day. There had been a heavy thunderstorm days earlier. The temperatures had dipped, and the air took on a crisp freshness I hadn't felt since April. My son and I padded along side by side through the woods. From the gravel road, we turned off onto a path that would lead us to the lake where we planned to set up camp. It was still late morning, which meant we had plenty of time.

My son told me he had dreamt in the car that we ate worms for dinner, the ones we had brought along to use as fishing bait. Then, as we walked along the path, he found a stick that looked like a sword. Soon after, he found another stick that looked like a sword, and in no time he realized there were sticks everywhere and that all of them looked like swords—but this didn't mean we had to carry all of them with us.

The heather that lined the sides of the path had turned red. The blueberries and raspberries had shriveled and dried up. My son found two bottle caps on the ground that he put in his pocket. Then he said he was starting to get tired. Around the same time, I began to consider there might be something wrong with our path. We stopped and looked at the map. Our location seemed to correspond to the terrain, but not completely, and I eventually realized that we were on the wrong track. Two almost identical paths led into the forest from our starting point and continued for a few miles, and we had chosen the wrong one. This path would not lead us to the lake. I scoured the map for another nearby lake to camp beside, but the landscape around us was flat and waterless and the path appeared to lead uphill the entire way. This particular terrain had no valleys, and therefore no lakes.

"We're lost," I said. I immediately regretted my choice of words. My son's expression was a mixture of amazement, disbelief, and fear. He has seen countless films on Netflix about people who are lost. All of the films end well, but before they do, the main character first has to overcome an unspecified number of difficult challenges that often involve fire-breathing dragons.

I saw the concern in his eyes but I pre-empted it. I said, "Relax, it's no problem. We'll just turn around and go back the way we came, and since we've already walked for such a long time, you can ride on my shoulders the entire way back."

And that's what we did. His fear dissipated. He sat on my shoulders and waved a stick that he pretended was a sword. He shouted into the forest that he was a knight and wasn't afraid of anything. And I was his horse. Onward! Onward! Here comes the proud Don Quixote of La Mancha and his steed, Rocinante, the latter so heavily burdened that he was a little bit worried about his joints and menisci. But the knight was unworried, and that was the only thing that mattered.

By the time we finally reached our campsite, I was completely worn out and my son was well rested. We set up the tent. It was a dome tent. Once the poles were in place and the tent had taken shape, I lay down on the heather and gave my son the task of pushing in the tent stakes and unpacking our things in the tent. He went about his duties with the utmost gravity. Hammered away at the stakes with a big rock, solemnly removed one object after the other from the backpack. Stowed everything away neatly inside the tent.

I watched him from the heather and thought about the overnight trips I'd taken with my father when I was young. We didn't have too many trips together—three, maybe four—but I can remember all of them. I loved to fish; my father couldn't stand it. Nonetheless, fishing was what we did together. Every single time. I remember the tent, a faded, green cotton tent that absorbed each drop of moisture until it was wet through. It was, in essence, the antithesis of a tent, but my father insisted it did the job superbly and we never replaced it with a newer or better one.

The morning at the lake in the woods turned into afternoon. We had eaten and played and waded and whittled. We had gone down to the water and put out our fishing rods with earthworms on the hooks, and then laid down in the tent and rested while we waited. My son said he wanted to go down to the water to check if he'd gotten a nibble. I said that was a good idea—it's been a while since we put out the lines, there might be a fish on there by now, a perch or maybe a trout—and I would stay in the tent and watch him through the opening. He didn't reply, but I could see he was happy about our agreement because he turned and walked through the heather, not the way he walks to his day care in the mornings, reluctant and trailing, or home from the grocery store, scatterbrained, aimlessly; he walked to the water in a different way, steady and confident. His entire being, all thirty-six inches of him with a crop of light hair on top, spoke of a small person who felt himself to be big— bigger perhaps than ever before. I stayed like that, lying in the tent, watching him through the opening in the flaps: I saw how he bent down and lifted up his fishing pole, pulled the line in carefully before he began to reel it in, examined the worm, threw the line out again, put his fishing pole down carefully, and secured it against a rock that was small, much too small. I saw all of this from the entrance of our tent, and I thought it was strange that he was down there while I was reclining up here, but this was simply how it would be because it's how it always is with anyone—one person doing their thing in one place while the other is off doing their thing somewhere else. There are times when I can't always see my son from where I am standing, at the playground for instance, and I knew there would come other times when he would be even farther from my sight. I thought about how I wouldn't always be able to keep an eye on him as I did now, from where I lay in this tent in the Nordmarka forest when he was four years old and I was forty-two.

By seven o'clock he wanted to go to bed. Partly because he was tired and partly because he thought it was exciting to climb into his sleeping bag. He had packed a little book and a tiny brown teddy bear. The book was an almost word-for-word translation of 101 Dalmatians, probably taken from the film. It was chock-full of plot twists and turns, and we read it four or five times. He wanted to keep reading, but I refused after that and said I would rather sing him to sleep. It had been a demanding day for him, with all the walking, naturally, but more importantly, the many new impressions.

I climbed out of the tent and sat down. I left the flap of the tent open so I could see him from where I sat. I thought that if he was anything like me, the two of us would recall this day very differently. For me, this was one day among many. I was formulating the trip as we walked—I would even go on to write a book about it; I had the overview and the experience, and the individual moments could be compiled into a mental card index that was functional and clear from beginning to end. But for him it was different. His memory was a sparsely furnished room, and this trip was purely sensory, wordless, and intuitive. He didn't even know where we were.

From where I sat, it seemed like a million years had passed since I was in my son's position. Out on an overnight trip with an adult in a place I'd never seen before in my life.

I am lying in a sleeping bag on a narrow bunkbed inside a primitive, off-grid cabin. It is autumn: September, maybe October. The cabin is uninsulated. I stare at the gray wall planks, dried and weather-worn from the wind and rain and warmth of the woodstove. It's evening. I am the only child there, and from out in the living room I hear the adults' voices. They have left the door open a crack. The warm light from the paraffin lamps flickers across the log walls. The wind whistles. The air outside is sharp and shockingly fresh.

The air inside is of a type I've never experienced before; it seems old, as if it's been inside for a hundred years.

It is the first time I've ever really been on a mountain, high up above the tree line, and I intuit this is something very special. All day long, the adults have been exclaiming how incredibly glorious it is to be here. Their pronouncements are general and bland, but as I lie there on the bunk I know I've now had my very own, individual experience on the mountain.

When I wake up the next morning, I pad out onto the stone slab that forms the cabin's threshold. A large flat stone covered in green lichen, icy cold and rough beneath my bare feet. And this is the point when the most prominent memory pops up: the first inhalation of air—mountain, fall, dampness—mixed with what I think must be the odor from the blue antiseptic liquid that was used in cabin toilets in the 1970s. Maybe also enhanced by the rustling from the willows and the rush of cold water from the stream running nearby, and some other things I couldn't recognize from where I stood. That was the first inhalation of air through my nose on this morning in 1978, and every time I've smelled something similar over all the years I've been out backpacking, I am immediately transported back to that little off-grid cabin on the mountain to which I have never once returned.

I sat quietly in the August evening. Dark clouds rolled in over the lake from the south. The surface of the water was still gray and unmoving, but it wouldn't stay that way for long.

Wind and rain were forecast throughout the night, and only a half hour later, the first gust arrived. It raked across the water forming small V-shaped waves, many distinct tiny puffs of wind moving in all directions and with surprising speed. When I was younger, I was convinced that these Vs were the result of fish swimming just beneath the surface of the water. I would cast out my line over and over again toward the Vs, but I never caught anything. I couldn't believe the wind could follow such a narrow course, so defined, so small. Now I know that it can, and that these miniature storm breezes are often the vanguard of larger wind systems.

The air grew colder. I went and got a beanie and jacket from the tent, swaddled myself in them, and sat down again. "I can see the shape of the wind on the water," writes Per Petterson in his novel *Out Stealing Horses*. And that is precisely how it is.

By ten o'clock it was dark. Waves slapped against the rocks down at the shoreline. I was cold and tired. I put spruce branches over the firepit to keep it dry. I brought all of our gear inside the tent. I tidied up and sorted everything, already setting out our clothes for the next day: fleece pullover and long johns for each of us, rain pants and rain jackets. And breakfast: water for my coffee and a yogurt drink for my son.

As usual, my son woke up first. Never in his entire four-year-old life had he ever slept beyond six a.m., regardless of when he went to sleep the night before. We've had many conversations about this early start, and I have often asked

him whether he might consider going back to bed for a little while. Each time he has replied that it's not his fault he
wakes up so early, and I've never been able to think of a
good rebuttal.

He propped himself up on his elbows and peeked out
over the edge of his sleeping bag. His eyes squinted, smooth
skin, summer-brown. Again, I could tell that he needed time
to figure out where he was. Then it dawned on him. He
peered up at the top of the tent, amazed at the many small
sounds coming from above. "Rain," I said. "That means we
have to plan things out really well before we head home."

The rain meant that everything had to be done at the right
moment and in the right order. We ate breakfast inside the
tent, packed our things, put on our rain clothes, and got
everything else ready to go. Then we unzipped the tent and
went outside. The only thing left to do was to tear down the
tent. We folded it and fastened it under the top flap of my
backpack. Then we began to walk.

The rain barreled down. We were soaked through before
we had made it even halfway back to the parking lot. My son
said he was getting tired again. Once again, he was allowed
to ride on my shoulders, which boosted his morale.

My backpack weighed fifty-five pounds, and my son, plus
his backpack, weighed forty-five. I was carrying one hundred pounds on my back. Our clothing was sopping wet
and my hiking boots slurped with every step. All of it was
propelled forward through the wet woods by my own body;

everything now rested on the office worker's back. In that moment, I suddenly felt very strong, strong enough that it was impossible to consider I might ever get tired.

I was a carriage through the woods. The rain fell soft and warm. The trees steamed. We were almost to the asphalt road and the place where our car was parked. We passed a cabin and a field. A fence ran along the side of the path. Suddenly I glimpsed a movement among the trees. Three hundred feet away, large bodies, grayish-brown and glossy. I stopped and stood completely still.

"Moose," I whispered, bending so my son could slide gently off my back.

I pointed in between the trees and signaled for him to stay silent. He stared. Then he turned to me and said in his high, piping voice: "Do you mean those horses, Daddy?"

# SEPTEMBER

## CAMP LIFE

===

"Nothing could compare to these empty autumn
days. (...) I roamed wherever I pleased, and nothing
was rushed or hurried. If I wished to pause and
smoke my pipe, I did so; if I wanted to climb along
the ridge of a faraway mountain because I was
curious what the other side looked like, I could. If
evening should suddenly fall, I would build a fire,
roast meat on a stake, and sleep where I was."

**HELGE INGSTAD,** *PELSJEGERLIV: BLANT NORD-CANADAS*
*INDIANERE (THE FUR TRAPPER'S LIFE: AMONG NORTHERN*
*CANADA'S INDIGENOUS PEOPLES)*

AUTUMN BEGAN ON the night of Wednesday, September 18. As usual, I noticed it when I went out to
get the newspaper from the mailbox in the
morning. This trivial task is, in my opinion, completely

underrated as a natural experience. You have just risen, and in this untarnished state you walk outside. The air wakes you up. Or nature does. Snow in the winter, birdsong in the summer. And on this particular Wednesday morning in the middle of September, I had been woken up by the rain. By plump, cold drops falling at a slant from the south that hit my face, and also by the yellow leaves that stuck to my shoes as I walked along the gravel path to our mailbox at the road. Autumn! said my mind, or maybe it was my body. I breathed in the unmistakable scent of cold air, decaying plants, and whatever it all is, all of it together, and wasn't there also a hint of wood smoke? It must have been from one of the neighbors, someone who all summer had been looking forward to this exact moment and could now finally take advantage of it to fire up their woodstove.

Three days later, on the day of the autumn equinox, I went to the woods again, eager to see how the conditions might be in there. Or rather, "out there" as Trude calls it; it depends on how you look at it. I was alone and glad to be. I was going to return to my campsite at the little pond. The plan was to spend the remaining four legs of my micro-expedition there. I didn't have any further plans than that, no particular activity I hoped to do or specific thing I hoped to see. No commitments, no goals, and no one to accompany me. I was thus free to decide on everything by myself, the grand flurry of civilized events had passed and I was once again my own master.

I slogged up the same inclines, along the same river, the same big lake, the same old logging road. It didn't matter to me in the slightest that I had already been there several times before, in fact it made the trail more interesting because I had become so familiar with these parts that I now knew where things were. Around every bend were new reference points. Protruding stones or the characteristic turns of the river, an old shed along the road that nature was slowly reclaiming. And the trees. Everywhere were trees I knew from earlier hikes but that looked changed since I'd last seen them.

I passed two trees standing off by themselves, both unusually tall and thin for their species. Maybe their growing conditions were optimal there: rich soil, enough water and sunlight to push them higher and faster than other trees of their kind. One of the trees was a pine and the other was a birch, and in February they had been covered by thick, gleaming frost and had stood out against the blue sky. Now the sky was hazy and undefined. The pine looked as it always had. The birch had changed.

I noticed these and many other things I hadn't seen since May, because I hadn't been there in June and August, and in July I had hiked to the pond from a different direction.

In May, the birch trees had been outfitted in freshly sprouted leaves. The green hue of the leaves was paler now. Some of them had turned yellow. Others had already fallen off and blanketed the ground. The chlorophyll was slowly being pulled from the leaves because the trees would need it to get through the winter. The trees would store that chlorophyll in their trunks and their roots and it would function, among other things, as antifreeze when the temperatures dropped. The colors that are revealed when the chlorophyll is withdrawn—for that is what actually happens, these typical autumn colors don't just come into being somehow during the new season—comprise the true pigmentation of the leaves. Yellow, red, brown, sometimes black. But, for the most part, birch leaves are yellow.

The blueberry shrubs had turned red, and everywhere I looked were rowanberries. Red-orange clusters so heavy that the branches holding them labored under the weight. There were fewer flowers lining the roadside at this time of year, but it had been the same in August. The big clichés of autumn—the enormous spectrum of colorful leaves, hoarfrost in the morning—belong to October. September is more of an either/or period. It is the month linking two seasons, the way that March provides a link at the opposite end of the calendar.

I peeled off from the logging road and climbed a steep slope of scree to get to the top of the ridge. It was hard going with my pack on, but soon I was up. I stopped to rest. Drank water and snacked on peanuts. The view spread out in every direction. It was overcast, but it didn't seem like it would rain. The sky was white. The temperatures had been rising over the previous week. It was about fifty degrees with no wind.

It was still more summer than fall. The new season hadn't yet triumphed over the old. In the mornings the air might be sharp and cold, but by afternoon the sun had burned off the moisture, infusing warmth into the atmosphere. It isn't always like that in September, but it had been this year.

I continued along the ridge. The Nordmarka contains many different types of forest but the southernmost portions are dominated by spruce trees. Many of the trees have been planted, and you can see this by the way they have been positioned in the terrain, with a geometry that reveals the hand of *Homo sapiens*. There are pockets of untouched nature there as well, protected areas known as primeval forests. But to reach these you must venture farther north. Nevertheless, throughout this year of my micro-expedition I had often taken to thinking that large portions of this forest area are relatively untouched. For example, where I found myself standing in that moment. There was no path that led to this spot, and there are tens of thousands of such spots in the Nordmarka forest, as there are in other forests around the world: countless anonymous flecks of nature that lack the characteristic features that always lure travelers to visit. A high summit, a river, a lake. The place I was standing had none of these, so how great was the chance that anyone had ever stood here before? Maybe an occasional hunter or two had sauntered across this very spot at some point during the last centuries. But more likely than not, no other human had ever stood precisely where I stood then. That was a nice thought. Perhaps not a very useful one, but it felt to me like a substantiation of my micro-expedition's underlying presumption: that everyone always thinks so big. Explorers want to do what no one else has done, or go to places no one else has ever reached. When environmental organizations and politicians discuss the protection of certain natural areas, these areas are always very big. They rarely think about small places. But if you do this, if you shift to the micro level, you will see that most of the forest still appears untouched by humankind. It takes hardly any effort to experience this. Turn off the main path, walk one hundred feet into the woods, pause, look around, and you will see that you are in a place that feels both untouched and completely undisturbed.

I continued my walk through the open terrain that is so typical up high. Sparse pine groves and bulging mountain rocks scattered about, blueberry bushes everywhere you look. This forest must have been old, I thought, because pines grow very slowly. Plus, there was hardly any soil, only rock, which offers scant nutrition to trees. If anyone were ever to ask me what my favorite type of forest is, I would reply: "Open pine forest in craggy terrain." It is an uplifting type of landscape through which to pass because light floods in from every angle, even on a cloudy day.

I arrived at the campsite around lunchtime and immediately recognized the signs of people having been there over the summer. This wasn't surprising exactly, since the woods are full of people in the summer and this was not an off-the-map kind of spot. Someone had tossed three beer cans into the firepit along with an emptied, crushed tin can, a clump of balled-up fishing line, and a waterlogged snuffbox. I didn't like it, this evidence of human disturbance, but I didn't have any choice. This campsite didn't automatically belong to me just because I had spent a handful of nights there throughout the past year.

On all of my trips, I had often come across trash left behind at various camping spots, and the fact that so many people apparently don't have a problem with lobbing their garbage into pristine nature really bothers me. It has to be one of the stupidest, most irresponsible deeds possible. It destroys nature and also the experience of nature for others. And there's absolutely nothing to be gained by it. There is no upside, as they call it in the private sector, other than, maybe, that you don't have to carry your own garbage to the closest dumpster. Carrying a tiny wad of fishing line can hardly be considered an effort.

If people can't even manage to pack out their own garbage when they are in the woods, can they manage anything at all? Strewn across the campsite were dozens of small, thin branches with withered leaves. Fifty feet away, at the edge of the bog, were two short birch stumps. The branches must have originated there. Which meant that someone had cut down these trees in the ugliest manner possible, by the looks of it using a small axe with a short handle—the kind that is often marketed as outdoor equipment but that is almost impossible to use because the handle is too short and thus the force of the blow is too weak to make a clean cut. The stumps were no thicker than an adult's upper arm, yet it looked as if it had taken hundreds of blows to hack through them. Bad gear, or else bad technique, or both. It was ugly, as if a beaver had been set loose on the trees to gnash away in a blind rage or in frustration over just how monotonous the life of a beaver can be.

I gathered all of the thin branches and broke them into equal-sized pieces. They had partly dried out through the summer and thus they snapped easily and would make good kindling. First, I lit a fire. Then I set up the tarp and my tent. This time, I put the tarp over my tent to function as an additional rain cover. As I carried out this task at which I was getting more and more efficient—not that it took me less time, but that I did it more calmly and with more precision—I kept an eye on the campfire, and every now and then I put another branch on. By the time I was done, the campsite was spic and span and every trace of the interlopers had been erased.

I stowed my gear inside the tent, blew up my ultrathin sleeping pad, unrolled my sleeping bag—an ultralight bag this time, but with a fleece inner bag that was supposed to increase the temperature inside. I took out my headlamp and a book, my cooking gear and food, and placed everything either under the tarp or inside the tent. Then I got out a package of hot dogs and lefse flatbread—which is a sort of potato tortilla that we Norwegians wrap around our hot dogs instead of buns—and whittled a stick to use for roasting.

At this point, the fire had reached the perfect temperature for grilling. I roasted and ate five hot dogs with lefse and drank a quart of water. Then I boiled water for coffee. I only bring a single pot along with me on trips and I use it for everything. I have no use for the fancy cook sets that you can get at outdoor stores, the ones that come with a sauté pan and a coffeepot and three or four pans of various sizes. All I need is one. This may be something I have already mentioned, but I'll say it again: my one camping pot and my tarp are the two objects in my life that I will never tire of talking about.

A lot of soot covered the pot. This is the price you must pay if you decide to boil water directly over open flames. Still, the coffee tasted good. When I had drunk my fill, I made sure that the embers were safely contained within the large rocks that formed the firepit. After lunch, I assembled my rod and reel and padded down to the pond to see if the trout were rising.

It was three in the afternoon. In four hours, it would be dark. The autumn equinox is one of many astronomical markers in the calendar year. The fact there are so many such markers reveals that people in the old days had a great need to organize the seasons and create fixed points amid all of the changes. The simple explanation as to why this exact day—which falls on either the 22nd or 23rd of September each year—is an astronomical anniversary is that it is one of two days in the year when night and day are of equal length, or to say it more precisely: the sun remains above the horizon for the same amount of time as it stays below it. The more complicated explanation has to do with the sun's position in relation to the equator, and to the earth's axis being tilted in relation to its orbit and to a lot of other factors that I have tried many times, albeit not very successfully, to grasp. I even went so far as to ask a professor of theoretical astrophysics to show me the process with hand-drawn diagrams, but even then I didn't quite get it, although I pretended I did.

Precisely six months to the day opposite the autumn equinox is the spring equinox, which falls every year on either March 20th or 21st. Although the light conditions are identical on these two days, the days on either side of each equinox move in opposite directions. In March, conditions grow lighter; in September, they grow darker. Yet once again there is a lag in the system, and the result is that temperatures in March are considerably lower than they are in September for the simple reason that March marks the end of winter, while September marks the end of summer.

I walked along the edge of the yellow peat bog as cautiously as I could, and I thought that a bog must be the component in nature for which the fall colors are best suited. A bog makes me think of autumn regardless of what time of year I see it. It is, at its heart, autumnal—yellow and damp—and if there is anything at all to this thought, it would have to be that the bog was in its element now and was heading into a season when it could be fundamentally and fully itself, without artifice or excuse.

I was thinking like a Romantic poet. I was Lord Byron of the Norwegian woods. I sat down on a rock under a tall, thin pine tree, on a headland at the center of the pond's long end. At the center of the pond, a trout was rising. It was too far away for me to cast, and the ripples were so tiny that I would never have noticed it if a wind had been blowing over the water. It was classic midge feeding behavior. They are so small, these midges, that the trout don't need to do anything other than rise slowly up to the surface and slurp them directly into their mouths. If there are a lot of midges on the surface, the trout can simply patrol the whole area just beneath the surface, sucking them in one by one. In that way, if you are a fly-fisher, you can sometimes judge which direction a fish is heading by the progression of tiny ripples. Then you can get ahead of the trout and put a fly in its path where you think it will go next. It is an exciting and challenging way to fish. And because the fish remains below the surface to feed, it means you never know how big it is until you have it on your hook. The smallest ripple might come from the biggest trout.

I got out my matchbox full of flies and selected one of the smallest artificial mosquitoes. Just as the mayflies and caddisflies do, midges also go through various stages of development, and trout will eat them at all of these stages. Larva, hatchling, and mature insect. I selected the mature insect, a tousled little thing that would float high on the water's surface, so high that it would almost look like it was hovering, which is exactly the way a real midge appears from below.

The trout I noticed was rising in circles at the center of the pond's otherwise still surface. I stood ready with my rod. I hoped it would choose to alter its course and swim closer. It was no simpler nor more complicated than that. No other fish were in sight. Only this one lone trout, so I was not exactly having to be selective, as is often agonizingly the case in the early summer months.

June is explosive with a great many mayfly hatches that attract lots of trout, which not infrequently leads to stress and haste and a lack of general oversight when fishing. In July and August all kinds of insects are on the water, ants and caddisflies and mosquitoes and moths and crane flies are abundant. September is the first month when the selection begins to narrow. For fly-fishers, this can be the time of purest happiness because it is easy to keep one's bearings. The sheer number of insects is less now. And the time during which a particular insect is on a trout's menu has grown shorter. The chance of snagging a trout, however, is greater. I imagine. This tendency increases throughout the fall season. It's even more apparent in October, and by November the insects buzz about only during a brief period in the middle of the day, and then only if the sun is warm and there is no wind. It is their final hurrah before the darkness and cold creep in, and you would be lucky to see a trout feeding at all.

I had already started to long for the solitude of autumn. The summer season had felt like it was too much of everything. There were too many alternatives, and I think I am the kind of person who was made for the fall. I like that it is a season free of events. I like the sense of reduction that takes over the woods, and the clear feeling of entering into a state of slumber. It is a time when you can pull back, take stock and tidy up in your own life, patch anything that needs mending, and find your footing. And after that, after you've recovered a bit of perspective, you can start to make plans for the next summer.

A midge is a robust little creature. It hatches in both still and running water, and its only requirement is precisely that: unfrozen water. It must have been what the white-throated dippers were feasting on along the icy edge of the river back in February. And was what the trout were sucking down from the top of the pond on this day in September. A half hour passed, and then the trout began to rise closer to where I stood on the shore. For once I was in luck. There were three or four ripples, and each one came a bit closer. After the fifth, I had an idea about where the fish was headed. I cast out. The artificial fly landed just about where I had hoped. The tippet, the thin line connecting the fly and the fly line, wasn't taut but I hoped it would be good enough. The trout rose again, even closer this time. Then, quite simply, it bit.

I'll admit it doesn't happen often. Midge fly-fishing on a flat pond is not the easiest thing one can do. The trout struggled in the deep, marshy water, but the hook held and the fish soon gave up. I lifted it out of the pond. It wasn't big, only half a pound at most. Its scales were dark brown, and it didn't have any red spots, only black. It looked exactly like the kind of trout that tend to live in dark, boggy ponds. I broke its neck and set it down beside me on a rock. I sat for a while longer, but I didn't see any other fish rising.

I fastened a large artificial caddisfly to my line, stood, and began blind casting along the shoreline. "Blind casting" is the term for what you do if you don't see any fish rising. Larger flies can be effective in getting the trout's attention, even if the fish are busy doing things other than nibbling on whatever is on the surface of the water. I walked around the pond, casting all the time along the shoreline. Caddisflies often move in jerky motions on the water, and I tried to imitate this movement. When I had walked almost entirely around the pond, a trout splashed. Trout behave differently when they feed on caddisflies than when they are going for midges. They jump on top of the fly and make a big splash, often so big and violent that you are later disappointed when you see how small the fish actually is. This one wasn't very big, but it was bigger than the first one. My fly caught strongly on the trout's upper jaw.

I rinsed off both trout in the pond before sauntering back up to the campsite. It was starting to get dark and I was hungry. I rekindled the fire and took out my food. I realized I should eat the trout immediately, but I wasn't in the mood for trout, which was hard for me to admit. I packed the fish into a plastic bag and saved them for breakfast the next morning. For dinner, then, I prepared my regular meal of bacon and mashed potatoes.

By eight o'clock, it was dark out, but the sky to the west was clear and bright. Gone were the clouds, and the stars began to emerge. I sat outside my tent wearing a light fleece jacket. The chill that had been in the air days earlier was gone. The temperature where I sat must have been above fifty degrees. But I knew it would be a cold night. And by the time I returned the following month, it would truly be autumn and conditions in the woods would have shifted entirely.

I sat soaking up the warmth of the campfire. Everything was prepared for the night and there was nothing left to do. I gazed around. I'd done it before, so I knew what was going to happen next. When the brain is left to itself—surrounded only by concrete, practical dimensions—that's when it really starts to work. And this is what camp life is. It is a basic, practical way of life, and I think it is probably the primary reason why people are drawn to it.

It's incredible how quickly our brains are able to adapt to new surroundings. This brain, which is used to talking on the phone and organizing tasks in the home office, putters about, taking in the campsite and devising possible improvements as if it had never done anything else. I felt a great urge to tidy something, to sweep the area under the tarp free of needles or any other organic material. I moved my backpack and cooking gear from their spot under the tarp, broke off a branch from a nearby spruce, and swept. Soon the ground was tidy and smooth as a ballroom floor. I put my backpack and cooking gear back. I returned to my spot in front of the fire, but hardly had I sat down than I realized I should probably devise a system for drying clothes, in spite of the fact that none of my clothes were wet.

Where my brain got that notion, I have no idea. I would rather have stayed quietly seated, staring intently into the flames, pondering eternity. I would rather have written poems, as Lord Byron supposedly did. Or Johann Wolfgang von Goethe. But I was unable to tap into that inner peace, and so I stood up again, snapped off a couple of long, thin rowan branches, and using my knife, peeled off all the bark so they would be clean and smooth. Then I positioned them, level and parallel to the ground between two trees, to make a drying rack. Of course, following that, I decided I needed to improve the campfire. Which meant gathering more wood. And then I needed to look for a rock to function as a little table for my trout breakfast the following morning, and after that, what could I do but bring over a round stump that could be used as a chair...

I should have gone to bed, but my body was restless. Something inside me was making a racket, and I am unable to ignore these kinds of practical challenges. I can be passive while a lot of things whirl around me, but god forbid you ask me to sit quietly when the matter at hand is a campsite in the woods. I see potential everywhere at every moment. It dawned on me then, as I pottered about in the light of the campfire, that I was touching on a very basic truth about my own brain. And perhaps about other people's brains. If I were to spend an entire year at my campsite, I'm afraid I might be in very real danger of erecting a whole city beside the little pond.

Before I finally crawled into my tent, I did one last thing that I had been considering for a long time. I prepared a campfire for the next morning. This fire had a very particular architectural structure that I had read about in a book and was eager to try out.

It is remarkable to me how much a single idea can develop if you take your time with it and don't just dive right in immediately. I first began to think about this when my children were small and I almost never had time to carry out my intended projects. The projects thus constantly changed over time, and from my extended consideration of them, improved, even though I hardly did anything but think about them. So I decided to spend the rest of my evening in September finding suitable branches to build my fire as well as possible.

The principle is a simple one: a normal fire gives off a lot of soot and pushes the warm air out in every direction, which means it takes a long time for the water to boil. But this special fire I had in mind would shoot the warm air straight up toward the bottom of my pot, like a Primus stove. You build this kind of fire by following these basic principles:

1.  Get four fresh, straight sticks, about one inch thick and one to two feet in length. It's important that you get freshly cut sticks so they don't burn up right away.

2.   Shape one end of each stick into a spike, leaving the other end flat across. Drive the pointy ends down into the ground like spikes, marking four corners so they form a small square that is slightly smaller than the bottom of your pot. Be sure that all of the sticks are flush on top.

3.   Arrange several small, dry sticks side to side on the ground in each of the four directions between the four upright sticks so that they are sticking out on every side of the square. Remember to place bark or some other quick-burning material at the base of the fire. Build up the sides of the tower on either side of the four fresh sticks and light the fire at the base.

The campfire looked promising. Before I went to bed, I cut off a few spruce branches and covered it up so it would stay dry if it rained. Then I crept into my tent, zipped it up, and snuggled down into my sleeping bag.

At five o'clock I woke up, ice cold and with an aching back. It was as I'd predicted; the temperatures had dropped in the night. My ultralight sleeping bag was much too thin, and the inner fleece bag, which claimed it would increase the temperature, hadn't lived up to its promise. In addition, my ultralight sleeping pad was punctured. It wasn't the first time that night. I had already been up several times trying to repair it by the light of my headlamp, crouching in my tent, shivering from cold as I stopped up the leak with glue and patches and then blew up the pad again before trying to fall asleep. But now it had gone bad. The air had leaked out as soon as I put my weight on it the very last time, and I had finally given up. I had thus slept with a large boulder across my lower back for the remainder of the night. The boulder stretched under the tent like the spine of a mountain and there was no getting around it.

I crawled out of my tent, stiff and cold and grouchy. I took out the water and coffeepot and matches, lifted the spruce branch off of my special campfire structure, and lit it at the bottom. The fire burned exactly as predicted. All of the heat was channeled upward to the bottom of the pot and soon my water was bubbling cheerfully. I guessed that it had taken the same amount of time as it would have with a Primus stove. I lifted off the pot and filled it with coffee. As it steeped, I used a stick to push the remaining pieces of the fire structure into the firepit. Then I filled it with dry bits of wood and soon the flames were dancing cheerfully there too.

The ground was warm and inviting to sit on, even after the cold night. I baked my bread on a stick. At home, I had mixed together some flour, salt, and a dash of dried oregano in a plastic bag. Earlier, I had filled the bag with bog water and massaged it into a dough. This I wrapped around a stick. These days, the Internet is filled with all kinds of hip "natural" recipes. On these websites the recipes are accompanied by photos of bearded young men in trucker caps sitting around a fire baking highly refined variations of stick bread, like bannock, and other traditional recipes made with ingredients I've only ever heard of but never tasted. This stick bread was the version I'd always known, scalding hot and slightly scorched at the edges, eaten with two trout seasoned with nothing but salt and pepper and then roasted skin down on the coals—all washed down with a swig of night-chilled bog water.

By seven o'clock the light had returned. The sun rose over the treetops and warmed me up on the mountain. Beside me, a group of ants struggled to transport needles that had fallen from one of the large pine trees. The needles were light brown, nearly yellow. The ants were working at a fast pace, almost frenetic, it seemed to me. One of them kept somersaulting over a pine needle that it obviously intended to bring back to the mound. But it couldn't figure it out: the pine needle was stuck and this fact appeared to infuriate the ant.

It got me to wondering why ants carry their dead. I'd often observed these processions on my trips, these small ants struggling beneath the weight of a dead companion with no indication that they might give up or ever consider the possibility. But what did they do with all of those fallen friends? Did they take them back to the mound and bury them there, or would they eat them? The answer to that question would mark the distinction between two diametrically opposed views of nature: the Romantic concept of nature as inherently good and humane and populated by animals with humanlike emotions on the one hand, and on the other, the biological view of nature as ceaselessly competitive, a space beyond morality, cutthroat, and populated

SEPTEMBER · CAMP LIFE    193

by unfeeling individualists. Something told me the ants belonged in this latter category.

When the fire burned out, I packed up my things and broke camp. I was leaving the site in better condition than I had found it, and this was a pleasant thought.

On my return hike, I met the bicyclists. I was descending the steep slope. They were on their way up. Their eyes were fixed on the ground directly ahead of their front wheel. Their expressions were determined. Of course, this had to do with the fact that they were biking as fast as they could uphill, but I couldn't keep myself from thinking that it also had something to do with the way they wished to be perceived. As goal-oriented, serious individuals with more important things to do than meander aimlessly in the woods. To me, they symbolized an achievement culture of almost comical dimensions. And I wish I could say that this cliché is not true, but it *is* true; that's exactly how they came across, these cyclists, as dead-serious individuals with only a single thought in their heads: efficiency. None of them said hello as they passed; they appeared to not even notice me, they simply pedaled more furiously. Nature for them seemed to be an arena for performance and achievement, for sport, not unlike a grass track or a skateboard ramp, a place where you can show off your stuff and I can show off mine, and we can all compare ourselves to everyone else and test our limits. I continued down the mountain, allowing myself in my state of self-satisfaction to think that for those who go out into

the wild, there seems to be an inversely proportional relationship between achievement and reflection. The more you
push to achieve, the less you really think. You won't get any
stories out of those wordless cyclists. They are too fixated
on their own sinewy bodies.

Later that day, sitting back in my home office, I switched on
my computer and opened my email inbox, expecting a flood
of new messages. Although the fall is less hectic than the
spring, there is still work to be done after all. I was expecting that I would need to concentrate and put in a full, hard
day's work in order to get back up to speed following my
most recent excursion in the woods. But I was surprised
by something that made me feel both happy and a little bit
superfluous: I had received only a single email while I'd been
away, and it was from an online store selling fly-fishing gear.
They were offering autumn flies at a reduced rate: "Don't
forget the midge flies," the email urged, "just remember:
autumn is mosquito time."

PART IV

# FALL

# OCTOBER

## A THEORY OF TWO SEASONS

"Autumn covers the earth, and everything
is suddenly too late and too early."

**ERLING CHRISTIE,** *HØSTLIG BEFRIELSE*

EVERY SELF-RESPECTING EXPLORER is eventually expected to reach some realization or other during their travels. This may be true of micro-expeditions as well, even if the expedition has no particular goal. I had long wondered what my particular realization might be, since I wasn't exactly probing uncharted territory. I had to date spent nine nights in this same forest over the course of one year. My experiences had been big and small, mostly small. If I had to point out one topic that had occupied my observations more than any other, it would have to be the continuous shift of light and temperature and the effects of these on the natural world.

Each time I went into the woods, something had changed. The weather, of course, but the weather is always changing; it is unpredictable and often surprisingly heedless of the seasons. The weather is an entire story in and of itself. But what had caught my interest on my overnight trips, and what I had had the great pleasure of observing up close, was the sum of all the subtle shifts in nature which, together, brought about a larger change and suddenly everything looked completely different. To an office worker, these tiny transitions are almost imperceptible: you only see the results of them. Nature is white in the winter. Then it turns green, yellow, brown, black—and then white again. For the unobservant, this transformation happens suddenly and abruptly. But for me, this year, things had been different. Already in October, before my year of micro-expeditions was over, I felt that it had been a success—assuming I didn't get eaten by wolves or fall prey to some other unpleasantness in the remaining three legs of my journey. But my aim had already been fulfilled. I'd had ample opportunity to observe the seasons up close, to study the tiniest shifts in nature, and to ponder them. The sum of all these ponderings resulted in what I, perhaps somewhat presumptuously, decided to call *a theory of two seasons.*

October was the poster child for autumn, the way that July had been the poster child for summer. I had been lucky with the weather throughout most of the year. The winter had been dry and cold; the summer, dry and warm. Only the spring had demonstrated any real downpours, but that was a long time ago by now and not something I thought too much about.

But all of that sumptuous weather can come at a cost. The lack of rain meant that the colors in the wild grew bolder and more intense throughout October, and I noticed that the leaves on the trees stayed for a long time this year before they fell.

September had been mild and sunny, and the beginning of October was more of the same. The temperatures got noticeably colder, but the sky was clear, and the sunshine made the fall colors pop, lending nature a patina that made the year itself seem overripe.

By mid-October, autumn was at its loveliest stage. I thought about going to the woods, but I had started to dream of winter and got it into my head that I should wait until the first snow had fallen. So I delayed my trip for as long as possible. I stayed in, working from my home office and dreaming of snow. What a moment that would be! To wake up one morning, pull open the zipper of the tent, and be the first person to witness the wondrous white particles falling from the sky. I dreamt of seeing the ground covered by a dry layer of new-fallen snow, of being the only witness to an entire generation of plants buried beneath all that white. Where it had only just been teeming with life, and where the terrain had been rugged and rigid and sharp with color, all would be white and pale and soft and rounded. And as silent as it can be only when new snow has fallen.

I dreamt about this throughout October and followed the weather reports closely. The temperatures rose and fell. Some days were cold and clear and then it would get cloudy and warm again. It wasn't until the end of the month that it began to get wet, which is what we are used to here in the fall. Cold rain. Dark by five p.m. Pitch-black asphalt, gleaming in the light of the streetlamps in the evenings. Brown leaves crumbling in the streets. Small, trickling streams on the sidewalks. In only a few days, autumn had taken on its old, familiar character again. But then the cloud cover broke up, the roads dried, and the sun poked its head out again. The temperatures rose. As the end of the month approached, I reluctantly had to admit that it probably wasn't going to be a white October after all.

I had been fantasizing about October since July. About the cold, clear air and the angled afternoon light that makes shadows grow longer and everything in the woods look different than at any other time of year. If the weather in October is good, I am inclined to call it the most beautiful month of the year. The temperatures and the air seem to be optimal for my particular body and mind. I never function better than I do in October; I am never sharper, more fit, or in a better mood.

The plan was to follow the same itinerary I'd taken in September, only this time I brought along extra clothing just to be safe. I also got out my winter sleeping bag from the shed so there would be no freezing this time around.

I left home in the early afternoon. The morning had been overcast but by the time I'd parked at the trailhead and pulled on my backpack, the cloud cover had broken up. Shortly thereafter, the sky turned a brilliant blue. A golden sun, and here and there a cotton-shaped cloud. No wind to speak of. Nothing but cold, sharp autumn air.

I was in my element as I hiked along the old logging road and on new paths, past two lakes I'd never visited before, across a ridge I'd never climbed, down in a hollow to a lake where I've often fished. I hadn't brought my fishing rod along. Fishing season was over as far as I was concerned, and I hoped to turn my thoughts to other things.

I decided the lake would be a good resting spot. I took off my backpack and unpacked my food. Two men in their sixties were sitting nearby, each of them on a boulder at the shoreline, eating their lunch. They had leaned their bicycles up against trees, their foreheads gleamed with sweat, and they looked so peaceful in the mild October afternoon. White undershirts and checkered button-downs with the sleeves rolled up. They looked like lumberjacks, the kind of woodsmen you sometimes see in black-and-white photographs from the old days.

I left the lumberjacks and continued on my way. October is the rutting season for many of the large forest mammals. They mate in the fall, spend the winter pregnant, and give birth to their young in the spring. It's the only conceivable solution in a subarctic climate like Norway's. Large mammals require large amounts of food to survive. Only in this way, on this schedule, can they hope for their young to grow strong enough to survive their first winter.

I didn't come across any large mammals, nor any small ones. But I did see plenty of birds, non-migratory birds I assumed, because the migratory birds must already have turned their beaks southward. Crossing one sun-drenched dale, I startled a flock of a kind of chickadee I'd never seen before. There were five or six of them, and they stuck together like a small band. Hopped from large rocks up into the trees, and from the trees back down onto the rocks. They had white and black stripes along their wings and light brownish-grayish heads. They were in constant motion, flying and hopping between the rocks and the trees, all the time keeping an eye on me. They flitted close to me and then retreated again. They were afraid, but not too afraid. Driven, I assumed, by that impossible combination of fear and curiosity.

My theory of two seasons had first begun to take shape in April. It had been warm during the day and ice cold at night, and I thought: What is the opposite of April? At what other time of year are conditions exactly the way they are right now? I arrived at the conclusion that it must be October, that October marks the transition to the cold period of the year just as April marks the transition to the warmer period. I thought about assigning March and September the same status, but then I realized this would be wrong. March and September can be called the first spring and fall months, respectively, but in my experience, these two months still belong to the time of year that preceded them, and which would soon end, and not to the period that was to come. March was winter. September was summer. But with April and October, it was different.

I had given a lot of thought to the seasons during my year in the woods, probably more thought than was healthy. I had truly tried to understand the seasons, to distinguish them from each other and to figure out when one switched over into the next. We take it for granted in the northern climates that there are four seasons, and in Norway we tend to be very proud of this fact. Winter, spring, summer, fall. Those poor, southern-hemisphere folks, we say among ourselves, those poor, seasonless saps.

But after a lot of reflection, I had arrived at the following conclusion: we don't have four seasons in Norway; we have two. Summer and winter. They are exact opposites. In the winter, it is minus five degrees Fahrenheit, and in the summer, it is seventy (or, in Norway, -20°C and +20°C). In the winter, it is dark for most of the twenty-four-hour cycle, and in the summer it is light for most of this cycle. On top of that, we have two obvious transitional periods, what we think of as spring and fall. It feels more correct to me to call these transitional periods than to call them seasons, because everything about them points to the seasons that are to come. Only at one point during each of these transitional periods is there any genuine seasonal moment to speak of:

April is the incarnation of spring.

October is the incarnation of fall.

The transitional periods last as long as the two seasons do. Winter ends in March, but the summer doesn't start until July. The summer ends in September, but the winter doesn't start again until December. The reason that these transitional periods are so long is that the difference in temperature between summer and winter is so great, particularly in the polar zones. In Norway, for example, there can be eighty or ninety degrees of difference between summer and winter. When we talk about seasons, we tend to think about something permanent and stable. Skiing in the winter and swimming temperatures in the summer. But seen in this way, only the months of July and August and January and February can satisfy such concrete thoughts about seasons. In Norway, we have three or four weeks when it is warm enough to swim comfortably outdoors, and three or four weeks in January and February when snow conditions are perfect for pursuing our desired activities. But before these weeks, and after, everything that goes on in nature is about transformation.

I continued along the western shoreline. Then I angled steeply uphill from the lake and into the woods and kept hiking until I reached the top of a ridge. I passed a small hillcrest that stuck up between the pine trees. I did what children do when they see something sticking up out of the terrain: I climbed it. The crest was covered with moss and thick lichen. I was drenched in sweat and I sat down on my backpack. The sun was ablaze, and I had to take off my fleece jacket and sit in nothing but my thin wool shirt. From my perch, I had an expansive view east over the forest, and I thought perhaps this would be a good spot for watching the sunrise. It wasn't too far now to my campsite near the little pond. I took note of the location and decided to return the next morning before first light. I wasn't quite sure what an October sunrise would look like. And what was more, when it would take place. A few days prior we had set our clocks back, and so I guessed it would probably get light sometime between seven and eight a.m.

I continued meandering along trails until three o'clock. Then I set my course toward the little pond.

Nature is a circle, and there was perhaps more to the cardboard circle we had cut out at primary school than we had truly known. It is only at the very top and the very bottom of this cardboard cutout that there is any stability. Everything else is primarily a transitional period. I've tried to figure out what characterizes these transitions, and I have arrived at the idea that the only stable factor is the light. No other predetermined factor exists in nature, only the light. Everything else does whatever it wants.

August and February contain hints of something new to come. Both are still within the framework of summer and winter, respectively, but it is during these months that the first signs that something else is on its way begin to appear. March and September are a little of both. Unstable and shifty.

It can be warm but it can also be cold. These months are the tipping points. Which side of the net the ball is going to land on is impossible to predict; it changes from year to year, from week to week, from day to day. April and October, in contrast, represent definitive turning points.

In addition, the light is not coordinated with the temperatures. Light precedes temperature, you might say; the light is the cause and the temperature is the effect. The soil and bodies of water must be warmed up and cooled down, and this takes time. Therefore, the lightest day of the year is not necessarily the warmest, which might occur a month later. And the coldest day of the year is not the darkest, but a day that comes a month after the winter solstice.

These thoughts and ideas had been slowly formulating in my mind throughout the first nine months of my expedition, and I finally wrote them down on my tenth outing, when I found myself in the transition between the two seasons.

No one had been to the pond since my visit in September. There were no tracks, no human touch, and a half-burned stick lay in the firepit precisely where I'd left it the month before. I felt relieved. This meant I wouldn't have to spend any time in the pitch black of night trying not to think up stories about dubious characters who had sat around this very same fire concocting dark plans.

I pitched the tent and tarp just as I'd previously done and stowed the gear inside. Then I leaned up against the mountain, soaking up the last rays of sunlight. Almost all of the leaves had fallen from the trees around the pond, and the floor of the forest was moist with a carpet of rotting foliage. The light fell at a slant through the landscape, lending a gravity and transparency to the natural elements. I could even clearly make out a tiny mosquito on top of the glassy surface of the pond, and in the final rays of light I noticed the wispy threads of spiderwebs wafting by on the air.

Dusk came already at four thirty, and with it the cold. I collected firewood, a few dry spruce twigs but mostly there was only wet and decaying wood to be found. With a few pieces of birchbark and a lot of prep work, I was able to get a fire started at last. The thing about a fire is that you think you've gotten it going when the larger pieces of wood start to catch, and you have for the most part, but it isn't a serious fire yet; it is only flames licking at the dry bits, and once those have burned up, which doesn't take very long, the fire dies down again. I knew this, of course, but I also tend to forget it every time. I am too optimistic: I don't prepare the fire well enough and I don't keep enough dry kindling piled up beside me. I always light the fire too soon.

This day was no exception, but in the end I was able to build up the kind of fire I needed, and the flames crackled and emitted their warmth. Outside the cone of light, complete darkness had descended by six o'clock. It was much darker now than it had been in January because there had been snow then. The sky was filled with stars. The Big Dipper became visible just overhead, and I wondered why this particular constellation always seems to pop up wherever I go.

You have only to turn your gaze upward and you will see those seven stars there, twinkling in their unmistakable formation.

When I went into the tent around seven o'clock, I noticed that frost had already begun to form on the fly. Which meant below-freezing temperatures overnight. This had not been predicted. Fortunately, I had brought along my orange sleeping bag and wasn't worried about being cold. I had also brought along a book, as well as two small bottles of Underberg herbal digestive for the sake of well-being.

I woke in the night to the sound of rain against the tarp. The forecast had predicted this. Yet, it's hard to grasp how quickly such a change of weather can happen. The sky had been clear and starry and the temperatures icy cold when I went to sleep, and the hours that followed had only gotten colder. But then, suddenly, the clouds had rolled in and the temperatures had grown milder while I slept.

I ate breakfast in the tent. The rain tapped steadily on the tarp. I dreaded going out again. I packed all of my things and stuffed them into the backpack. Then I put on my thick clothes, my shell jacket, and finally my rain pants. At last, I crawled out of the tent, broke it down, and set my course for the viewpoint where I had been the previous day.

I was nearly certain I was the only person hiking through the Nordmarka forest at that very moment—an ordinary day—at six in the morning on the cusp of a new season. The October rain was ice cold. A thick fog layer sat on top of the spruces. There was scarcely any light. Undeterred, I continued on to the viewpoint. In my pack was a full bottle of bog water. The stove and gas canister and matches were directly under the top flap of my backpack. If there was to be no sunrise, I would have to get by on coffee. As I walked over the reindeer lichen and moss through the saturated forest, I realized the transition from September to October had been much greater than I had been prepared for. It was a warning of what had become an inevitable effect: that the cold would win over the warm, and that we were definitely at the threshold of a new season.

# NOVEMBER

## THE LAST MAN ON EARTH

"Most feelings motivate action, one cannot want before one has felt. Feelings such as nostalgia and its emotional relatives—sentimentality, longing, and melancholy—function as deactivating. Do such emotions have any place in a biological scheme?"

DAG O. HESSEN, *NATUR: HVA SKAL VI MED DEN?*
*(NATURE: WHAT DO WE WANT WITH IT?)*

CAN'T REMEMBER EVER having spent time in the woods in November before. I've tried to recall an instance, tried to think of a reason I may have had for going. A natural phenomenon that takes place only at that time of year, or a late-fall activity best carried out in the woods. I've racked my brain. But I haven't been able to come up with anything. Nothing happens in the woods in November as far as I'm concerned. Therefore, this penultimate leg of my micro-expedition is both the least eventful and the most exotic of all the phases.

I'll try to be brief. It seems the appropriate thing to do when you're talking about November, this month that appears like a void on the calendar. In nature, all visual signs of autumn have been erased by the time it comes around. The leaves have all fallen, the migratory birds have all flown south. The insects are nowhere to be seen. The fish have stopped rising. Mating season is over. All the plants in the forest have withered. The amphibians have gone into hibernation. And some other creatures have migrated closer to the cities.

The night of November 11 was the first night of frost. The children immediately got their tongues stuck to the metal banister outside, and I thought about how certain human tendencies never seem to self-correct through evolution. The roads became glass-like surfaces. A thin film of ice coated the asphalt, making it completely impassable. Temperatures dropped below freezing for a week and then got warmer again. The sun shone for the few hours that it circled above the horizon; the ground thawed and turned muddy for the umpteenth time that fall.

And I have to admit: the shorter days and lower temperatures did nothing to make me want to go to the woods for the eleventh time that year. It was that season when it felt wiser to remain indoors. To sip tea. To stoke the fire in the woodstove. To watch TV and read books. Every time I thought about the upcoming hike, the primary feeling I had was one of unpleasantness. I lacked the enthusiasm I'd had at the start of my expedition. It had been colder then, and in addition there had been three feet of snow. Nevertheless, or perhaps precisely for that reason, I had been eager to spend the night outside. Back then I'd had something to prove, but I wasn't as curious anymore and I didn't think November would have anything to offer that I hadn't already experienced in October. The only things that came to mind were darkness and physical discomfort.

If it didn't snow soon, December would most likely be just as dark and dreary, since these two months resemble each other in the natural world. All of nature's annual tasks had been wrapped up, the decomposition was complete. The only thing left was for the snow to fall and cover everything up, but when this might happen was anyone's guess.

I dreaded my trip. I didn't tell anyone that I was dreading it, of course. Throughout the year of my micro-expedition, more and more people had started to ask me for tips about where to go and how best to spend the night in the woods, and a lot of them wanted to know what kind of gear was needed. I had also received a lot of questions from people wanting to pursue a similar undertaking. On several occasions, I'd started to notice that people spoke to me with a measure of respect, as if I knew something they did not. For a moment I worried that I may unwittingly have become the reluctant leader of a born-again movement. Maybe I imagined the whole thing. Maybe I mistook respect for people's uncertainty and amazement that I would venture out on such lonely overnight treks. I didn't know for sure, but I got it in my head that I should try to appear as restrained as possible and under no circumstances give the impression of doubt or weakness. Therefore, whenever anyone asked how my micro-expedition was going, I immediately replied that it was going great and that I was really looking forward to spending a night alone in the woods in November precisely *because* it was so cold and dark.

The end of the month fast approached and in spite of my increasing reluctance, I managed to select a date for the hike. By this time, the darkness was all-encompassing. It wasn't yet light in the morning when we dropped the kids off at day care and at school. It was already night outside by the time we sat down to an early dinner. But then something happened. The temperatures dipped below freezing again, and the cloud cover remained. Then came the snow. It wasn't much, but it was something. An inch of freshly fallen snow, and the hills were already frozen which meant that it stuck. The snow created a thin, brittle layer across the lawns of all the villas and the small roads and lit up the landscape and made everything seem brighter and more cheerful. Gone was all my irritation about muddy shoes and wet jackets. And most importantly: this little meteorological event gave me the push I needed to get up off my sofa and go out into the woods for the second-to-last time that year.

The logging road was as hard as the floor of a squash court. I had gotten out my Iditarod boots from the shed and wondered whether the creaking noise would still be there. It wasn't. My boots were as soft as butter on the hard surface of the ground; a half-year in the shed had apparently worked wonders.

I hiked up the slope. This time I decided to head straight for my usual lunch spot. I was curious what it would look like there in November. Afterward, I planned to continue on to the pond where I would set up my tent and go to bed as early as possible. I had gotten up extra early that morning in the hope that it would make me feel tired earlier in the evening. To tell the truth, I was still hoping to put this part of the journey behind me as soon as possible.

It was another ordinary day. I didn't expect anyone else to be in the woods, and I didn't cross paths with anyone. Nor were there any movements to be seen, any sounds. The little snow that had fallen lit up a gothic landscape dominated by tones of gray. It felt like walking around in the ruins of summer. As if I were a character from Cormac McCarthy's book *The Road*, plodding around a burned-out site after the catastrophe. I was the last man on earth. A void of sound, movement, signs of life. I knew there are things that happen in nature in November: a kind of important fundamental work takes place, preparations for the following spring. Among other things, this is when most flowering buds form. Then they wait through the winter, ready to burst out when the light and warmth signal it is finally time. All of this work was taking place around me, but these happenings were hidden from sight and they did little to make my hike more enjoyable.

At my lunch spot, however, were a few new things of note. The water had not frozen yet, and ice hadn't even started to form along the edges of the lake. I looked for, but didn't see, any of the white-throated dippers that were there in the winter; however, a few crows perched in the naked birch trees on the opposite shore. They lifted off and landed again several times. I could hear their *kaa, kaa*-ing, like an argument. The sight of the crows against the white backdrop of the sky added to the atmosphere of dissipation and demise.

I continued my ascent. Reaching the path that veers off from the logging road toward the pond, I was met with a surprise. The thin snow was completely smooth and undisturbed. No human being had yet passed this way, and no animals either, although it had been two days since the snowfall. Maybe surprise is too strong a word: the situation was pleasing. I did the same thing I'd done in March. Jumped out as far as I could from the bank to under the big spruce trees in order to hide my tracks. From there, I continued on across the frozen forest floor.

When I reached the little pond, I was greeted by another pleasant surprise. The entire body of water had frozen, and on top of the ice was a blanket of newly fallen snow. I immediately perked up. This was a small shift in a positive direction since last I'd been there. If you are going to spend the night alone at a pond in the woods in November, it's not hard to imagine the world of difference between a frozen pond blanketed with a layer of fresh, fluffy white snow and an open pond stirring with dark, oily water.

Throughout the fall, I had been reading a book written by biology professor Dag O. Hessen entitled *Nature: What Do We Want with It?* I had brought this book along with me now. It was full of ideas and points of view regarding nature and the human relationship to it. At the most basic level was a clear environmental perspective. Hessen provided good, fundamental reasons for why we must take care of nature: that we are dependent on it, not only to give us food and other necessary raw materials but also because it provides us with experiences. A researcher and outdoorsman, Hessen is an academic who also possesses an emotional connection to nature. This connection, he wrote, was one of the most important factors that had prompted him to write the book, that he, in spite of having been educated within a strict scientific discipline in which evidence was a condition for every theory, nonetheless associated nature with feelings. Hessen wrote insightfully about why he had always felt drawn to nature, to landscapes, and to the many various natural phenomena. And in the passages that spoke directly to me, perhaps especially because I was reading the book in the fall, he wrote about the emotional trinity: melancholy, nostalgia, and yearning.

*Nostalgia is an interesting feeling because it doesn't have a rational cause. Feelings most often function as evolutionary compasses for the best choices: hunger, desire, anger, joy, fear, love, aggression—all of these are neurological processors directed by hormones and pheromones in the brain to the end of an evolutionarily speaking "right" choice. (...) Nostalgia, on the other hand, has no apparent utility; it is as useless as melancholy.*

Why do these feelings exist within us if they don't serve an evolutionary function or purpose? asks Hessen. They are not productive emotions, they do not prompt action, in fact it's most often the opposite. A nostalgic person is, by definition, inactive. Someone who dwells on what has been even when it is far too late to do anything about it. From a biological perspective, such an activity leads nowhere. Just imagine a moose that, instead of eating to build up fat for the winter, lies down in November and starts pining for all of the magnificent summer evenings spent at the pond. Imagine this moose stays there, reminiscing on that fabulous season past and wondering what it's about, all of this toil and striving, maybe also asking itself the most basic questions of a moose's existence and, in the worst case, arriving at the conclusion that existence is totally futile. If a moose ever started to do something like that, nature would quickly extinguish it from the ranks. That moose would face a reckoning at the very first crossroads, or else starve or be eaten, forgotten long before the spring.

I pitched the tent in the usual spot but made sure to avoid the sharp boulder that had punctured my sleeping pad back in September. Then I put all my things inside the tent: the

Hessen book near the head-end; a cheap but thick sleeping pad this time, good old closed-cell foam; and on top of that my down sleeping bag. After setting everything up for the night, I wandered down to the pond to look at the ice. The pond crackled as it had in April. The snow was light and dry. Here and there a spire of golden straw stuck out of the ice, and there were a few spindly bird tracks or perhaps they were from a mouse. I walked back to the tent and got out the dry birch wood I'd brought along. It was two o'clock. In only two hours it would be dusk.

The conditions were closing in, there could be no doubt about that. Anyone who writes knows that sadness is easier to write about than happiness. As I sat there, alone with my notebook on my lap, I felt the whole situation was forcing reflections that I didn't have. Sitting in front of the fire, I tried to formulate something clever that I hadn't already written three or four times before.

The evergreen forest was dark, even if there was still light in the sky. But the light was flat and dead. It was merely there. It didn't fall on anything, there wasn't a ray of any sort; it didn't cast shadows or give off a sense of depth the way it can on clear autumn days. It was impossible not to feel a kind of melancholic longing. If I'd had company, if I hadn't been alone, things might have been different. And although I no longer felt afraid of being alone in the woods, I felt lonely and, in a strange way, exposed. I could speak but there would be no one to hear me. There was no one else right where I was. Of course, I could always dial someone on my cell phone, provided there was coverage, but it would feel unmusical and shrill to talk on the phone in a place like this.

There was nothing particularly remarkable about the campsite. It was ordinary bordering on boring. Still, I was captivated by the thought that this place looked as it always had, and every time I thought about this, it seemed more and more incredible. That this place, with its rocks and mountain and peat bog and pond, or the pine tree down on the headland where I had caught the trout in September, that all of it had always been in the same spot. Pine trees grow older—the one down near the pond might be a hundred years old, possibly more for all I knew. A seed had once fallen in the soil of that headland, maybe around the same time in history when the union with Sweden was dissolved, maybe during the Napoleonic Wars. Most likely it came from one of the surrounding pines, maybe one that was dead now and had sunk to the bottom of the bog and vanished. The seed had spiraled down as it fell, and up grew a green sapling. It grew into a little pine tree, and with the years it got much larger. And always it stood in this place, with a view to the pond, quiet and unmoving, day in and out, year in and out.

If nostalgia doesn't have a purpose, why do we humans always seem to have this feeling of sadness in the fall months? Is it the darkness, the rain? Or the reminder of the inevitable fact that everything perishes, everything withers and dies?

If the biology professor Hessen said that the feeling of nostalgia could not be explained evolutionarily, I was inclined to believe him. I wasn't about to challenge his theory. Nevertheless, I thought, it had to be good for something, this feeling of yearning. I felt it myself, and always most intensely in the fall. It manifested as an undefined longing for something that had once been but was no longer there. It had to do with memories, and with my idea of who I was and who I had been. And in this sense, I differed from the fictional moose I'd dreamt up, but also from all the other beings around me. For this is a characteristic of humankind; it is the very definition, nearly, that we carry within us an idea of who we are and our place in the world. We have memories, but a lot of other kinds of animals have memories. What distinguishes us from animals is that we have a self, as it's referred to in psychology. We have a sense of who we are and who we are not, not only as isolated, biological creatures but also in relation to everything around us, both fellow humans and nature.

"Nature hardly knows what a landscape is," writes the literary scholar Henning Howlid Wærp in his doctoral thesis on nature poetry. A chickadee pecking a seed loose from a pinecone doesn't pause to consider that it is a chickadee pecking a seed loose from a pinecone. It has no idea of itself in the world; it has not been blessed with the ability to picture itself from outside of itself. Or cursed with the ability. It does not possess the ability to reflect, and thus, in a certain sense, it has no free will. It acts from a collection of basic instincts that tell it what to do, when, and how. And that's it. Such a life does not contain the fertile soil for nostalgia that human lives do. We have a free will. We are constantly choosing: Should I do this or should I let it be? Through our many choices, we slowly stake out a course for our lives, but this course could always have been another—maybe it should have been another. There are no answers but there are thousands of questions. Doubt always has the richest growing conditions, and the fall—maybe November in particular—is the perfect setting in which to slip loose this doubt. And with it the nostalgia. And the melancholy. And the yearning. The French philosopher René Descartes' well-known phrase "I think, therefore I am" could also have been "I regret, therefore I am." Or "I yearn, therefore I am."

By four o'clock it was dark. It was brisk outside but overcast. Every source of light had been swallowed up, but the snow made things slightly less black. I sat in front of the campfire until it burned to embers. Since there was no more danger of forest fire now, I left the glowing coals in the pit. I crept into my tent and crawled into my sleeping bag, took out Hessen's book, and hunkered down for four hours of reading before bedtime.

I ate peanuts and read about nostalgia. I thought, The fact that this feeling is such a central part of our emotional register must mean that it has some sort of function, doesn't it? I could only speak for myself, as usual, but from where I lay in my tent, it seemed that this feeling had something to do with the sense of time passing. November was a constant reminder of the brevity of life, and in this respect was an entire month perfectly suited to the feeling of nostalgia. But what could the function be, from a biological perspective? It must be that nostalgia forces a form of reflection, a kind of mental register of life so far and a preparation for the life that is ahead. Preparation for the choices to come, so that they can be made on a better basis than earlier choices, which might serve to continue the species. Nostalgia has to do with reason. And reason is humankind's foremost advantage in the struggle for existence.

I read Hessen's book for quite a while. At nine o'clock, I put the book into a little pocket on the inside of the tent and switched off my headlamp. It was very cold. I had to wear my ski cap and pull my sleeping bag tight around my head to stay warm.

I am just like my son, or he is like me. I always wake up early regardless of when I go to bed, which means that I am always tired early in the evening. Such a state is very beneficial when you are alone in a tent in November.

I fell asleep around ten o'clock and woke up several hours before the light had returned. It didn't matter. It was morning. Everything was simpler then, and any hints of melancholy had dissipated. I had already prepared the stove, water, and coffee the night before. All I needed to do was zip open the tent, lean outside, and fire it up. In with coffee. And then I could simply lie back down in my sleeping bag and doze for a little while longer. Then back up again, pull on my clothes, crawl out of the tent, and feel the cold November air against my face. My body was heavy and stiff. I had to rattle it into motion, but after a while the warmth came back into my limbs. It always does.

I left the campsite the way I'd found it when I arrived. Now, I said to myself, there is only a single day left in the woods and then this micro-expedition will be history, one more experience on which to think back with feelings of nostalgia.

I walked quickly to keep warm. It still was not light. There was nothing to hear but the sound of my own foot-steps. I thought of our four-person home. I looked forward to returning there and going inside. Not because of the warmth but because of the light. Nostalgia is fine in small doses, and maybe it has its value. But it can easily get to be too much, and fortunately it is a feeling that doesn't propagate very well where there's an abundance of light.

# DECEMBER

## THE END AND THE BEGINNING

=====================================

"And human, here I think of you. Of every other
creature alive in the world, you are born to
nearly nothing. You are neither good nor evil,
you are called into being without an intended
aim. From the mist you come and to the mist
you return again, so imperfect are you."

**KNUT HAMSUN**, *ON OVERGROWN PATHS*

NATURE IS A circle. It has no beginning and no end.
It neither goes somewhere nor comes from some-
where. Light follows darkness; cold follows warmth.
Spring, summer, fall, winter. And then spring again.

Nature has its own changeless logic, and in the midst
of this live humans. We exist for some years and then we
die and others take over. Ours is a struggle against nature.
We shield ourselves from it as best we can, hold it at bay

outside our cities, outside our houses, outside our bodies. And yet, we dream about nature and it so happens that we venture into it, though preferably only when it is mild and predictable. When nature rages, we cower in fright and ask ourselves what can be done to stop it.

A Friday at the end of December. One of the year's darkest days. The snow that had fallen in November did not stick around. A few days after my November return from the woods, the rain and warmer temperatures came back. Ever since then it had been gray and wet outside. The worst imaginable conditions for spending a night in a tent.

It is morning. I am seated on a large rock in the southeastern corner of the Nordmarka forest. I have woken up for the twelfth and final time in the woods this year. Now it is over. In a little while I will get up and amble back home, say hello to Trude and the kids, exaggerate when they ask how cold it was, hang up my tent and sleeping bag to dry like I always do. Then I will pack them away to store in the shed along with all the other gear from my pack. The knife that is too big and has too many features, and is thus neither good for whittling or chopping. The headlamp that chafes at my forehead and always falls down so that only my stomach is lit up. All the wool and fleece clothes I've come to love. The puffy snow pants that warm me up even when they're wet, and the gaiters I have never once used. PrimaLoft and Gore-Tex, my thermos and storm lighter. The Iditarod boots that improve with each step, and my sleeping pad—the damned sleeping pad, neon yellow and pretentious, so superlight and super thin that it punctures more often than not.

All of this and much more than I thought I might need back in January, but which I never even took out of my backpack. What was I thinking when I bought this stuff? Did I think I'd be gone for a long time? Did I think I was venturing out into wilderness so perilous that all of this gear and equipment was actually going to be necessary, maybe even vital to my survival? Why, for instance, did I buy that compressible travel towel?

The answers are in my mind somewhere, but I can no longer access them. It's just as well. Because now they will be swept into the little shed together with all the other stuff, and there they will stay for a long time until I haul them back out again.

It is nine a.m. but still not very light out. The temperature is just at the freezing point and it is raining. And windy. I can hear the gusts through the treetops even if I can't see them. It has been raining all night long. Everything is saturated.

When I arrived at the campsite beside the little pond yesterday afternoon, I knew I had one hour before the darkness set in. The rain was icy cold. It was all very uncomfortable. But if there is one thing I've learned throughout the year, it's this: in the woods, there is no one to help you and nothing is going to get better unless you do something about it. Everything has to be done in the right order and at the right time, no matter how unpleasant it all is.

I mumbled, "First things first," breathed warmth on my fingers, and got out the tarp—this rectangular tent cover on which I've come to depend. It can be fastened to anything and will provide shelter from the wind and rain. A tarp is the simplest and best piece of outdoor equipment I have ever owned. It's also one of the cheapest. I've taken it with me on countless hikes and backpacking trips over many years, but it remains in exactly the same condition as ever, no rips, no holes, even though it's been strung up dangerously close to the fire on a number of occasions.

I strung up the tarp between four pine trees before putting up my tent beneath it. My tent is the kind where the inner tent body has to be set up before you can assemble the rainfly, a sequence that is less than optimal when it is raining out. I've sometimes had to bail water out of my tent. There's nothing charming about this, not even in retrospect.

This is why I now pitched the tent under the tarp. I couldn't hammer the stakes in because the ground was frozen. But the tent is freestanding and, in my opinion, dome tents like mine are the best sort for general outdoor recreation. They are freestanding and have a lot of headroom, much more headroom than in a so-called tunnel tent. Headroom is a big advantage if you have to spend several waking hours inside the tent. Which is what you should expect if you are going to spend the night alone in the woods in December.

I realized that trying to light a fire would be pointless. It was raining; it was blowing; I would never succeed. By three it started to get dark. I crawled into the tent, took off my wet clothes, and put on dry ones. The water had seeped into my backpack and everything was wet, but I had stored the extra change of clothes in a plastic bag. Then I set out to dry the wet clothes for the morning, because rain had been predicted for the next day too. My dome tent has some useful drying hooks at the top. I hung up the wet clothes and decided that I would shove them down inside my sleeping bag when I went to bed. My underwear was wet too. It was cotton. I hadn't bought any other kind yet, and in that moment I could hardly believe I'd made it that far without having done so. I decided it was one of the things I would do as soon as I got back to the city: purchase wool underwear that I could enjoy for the rest of my life. I took off my cotton underwear and put it outside the tent. It would never dry. Perhaps I could burn it the next morning in the fire. If, that is, it was dry enough to light a fire.

By four o'clock, it was so dark out that I had to turn on my headlamp. Back in the city, people were still at their jobs. And here I was, crouching in the pitch darkness in the cold, forsaken forest. What do you do when you are alone in a tent with seven hours to kill before bedtime? You read. And eat. And read. Then you tidy up the few things you've brought along. Eat more. Read more. And then tidy up again, even though there's nothing to tidy. And this is what I've come to experience many times throughout the year. It isn't boring. Not at all. On the contrary, in fact, time passes incredibly quickly and with every hour you become more and more acclimatized and suited to this silent and completely inactive lifestyle.

On each of the twelve overnight trips to the woods, I had brought along a selected book. I hadn't read all of them. Particularly in the spring and summer there had been other items on the agenda and I had only spent a handful of hours under the tarp, hours primarily for sleep. It was different now, though; in December I could read what amounts to almost two full working days' worth of literature.

For this last leg of my micro-expedition, I had saved one of the bonbons of outdoor nature writing: Henry David Thoreau's *Walden—Or Life in the Woods*, the bible of natural Romanticism and a book with fresh editions still constantly being printed more than 150 years after it was first published. The book follows the two years Thoreau spent in a self-built cabin next to the small pond named Walden, just outside his hometown of Concord, Massachusetts. I'd read it before, but a few years had passed since then.

I snuggled down into my sleeping bag and started to read by the light of my headlamp while the rain drummed down onto the tarp. The temperature hovered around freezing. The snow from November was gone. If I was lucky, the temperatures would drop overnight and the cold, hard rain would turn to fine white snow.

At seven o'clock, I switched off my headlamp and pulled the sleeping bag over my head. There's a lot you could say about Thoreau. A lot has been said. Some quotations from his book are very well known; for example, that he wished to live "deliberately." Which is a lovely desire that I imagine most people share. I'm not sure how many people read the entire book nowadays; it is somewhat punctilious, but it is easy to read and engaging and the message is clear: the lust for money and possessions ruins people. In pursuit of what people misinterpret to be the good life, they forget to live and they forget that this life, which they are in the process of frittering away, is the only one they have.

Even if Thoreau didn't use the term "wage slave," he'd certainly have nodded knowingly if he'd heard it. His primary aim for moving alone to the woods was to break away from the capitalist system, instead living according to his own simple economy. Rather than working for a particular number of hours, receiving a salary, using the salary to buy a train ticket, and then taking the train to a desired destination, Thoreau simply went there by foot. The time he saved by not working all those hours to save up the money for the ticket meant he arrived earlier. By consuming less, he reduced his dependency on money. He didn't have a job, and he spent his time doing what he wanted most to do, which was to think and write and spend time outdoors.

Thoreau must have been quite an oddball. He doesn't come across as a typical nature Romanticist; rather, he seems like someone who is very concerned about finances. Thoreau's main message to his fellow Concord citizens, on whom he bestowed little honor, was that they were throwing away their lives by working so much in the pursuit of money to buy ever more stuff. They were slaves of commercialism, wrote Thoreau. He himself was both moralizing and smug. Among other things in the book, he detailed the budget for all of his expenses related to the construction of the cabin. The total amount was $28.12, and he didn't try to cloak the fact that he was exceedingly proud of this number. One of the line items stated: "Chalk, 0,01$." Before falling asleep, I thought if only he'd known the price of an orange sleeping bag.

When I wake up, it is just as dark out as when I went to bed. The rain is still hammering against the tarp. Which means the temperatures did not, in fact, drop during the night. It won't be a white morning after all. I check the time on my phone. It's 4:30 a.m. but I feel wide awake and rested. I take out my Primus stove and the water bottle and start to boil coffee by the light of my headlamp.

I use *Walden* as a table. I think Thoreau would have approved of this. The book is dog-eared from the condensation in the night; everything inside the tent is wet. My sleeping bag too, but not the inside. The wet clothes I shoved down into the sleeping bag before I fell asleep are still wet.

Condensation is the tent-dweller's biggest problem during the winter months. How best to avoid condensation has proven to be the greatest puzzle for tent manufacturers and explorers throughout the ages. Having an inner tent body helps, but only somewhat. I have spoken directly with the Norwegian polar explorer Børge Ousland about this very issue. He solves the problem by sleeping inside a garbage bag inside of his sleeping bag. The moisture condenses inside the garbage bag but keeps the inside of the sleeping bag dry. Of course, the thin wool long underwear that he sleeps in gets damp, but it dries out quickly on his body. Ousland knows his stuff. There may not be any other living Norwegian who has survived as many nights in a tent in a freezing climate as he has.

I still have half of a normal working day left before it's light. After drinking my coffee, I continue to read Thoreau. I don't think we would have gotten along all that well, he and I, and maybe there is a reason as to why he was still single at my age. I never would have been able to live with his constant, falcon-like gaze over my shoulder: Are you really going to have *two* pieces of cheese on that piece of crispbread, Torbjørn? Don't you think one is enough?

Thoreau insisted on living alone in his little cabin. He claimed to spend no less than four hours out of doors every day, and only a person who thinks primarily about himself is able to make such a claim. Rumor has it that Thoreau's mother, who lived in Concord, only a short jaunt from the cabin, took care of his laundry.

There is something prophetic about Thoreau: he issues praises and rebukes interchangeably. He was only a few years younger than I am when he wrote *Walden* and even though he writes like an antique, there is nonetheless something that shines through that reveals he hasn't lived for very long after all. Thoreau has the greatest imaginable faith in himself. No one on this earth has more faith in themselves than young men, which is perhaps why young men are overrepresented among those who decide to break with civilization and live freely and purely in the wild. Chris McCandless in Jon Krakauer's book *Into the Wild*. Timothy Treadwell from Werner Herzog's film *Grizzly Man*.

After four hours, I have tired of both the tent and Thoreau. I pack all of my wet gear, shove it down into the backpack with considerably less care than when I packed it at home. Everything will have to be washed and dried anyway when I get back. Then I pull on my wet clothes from the day before. It is incredibly difficult to put them back on but I force myself to do it, and at last I crawl out of the tent and take it down too. Then I clamber up onto the boulder to wait for the dawn.

From the boulder there is a view out over the little pond. It is still covered in ice but now a thin layer of water sits on top of the ice. The few spots of snow form unusual circles on top of the water. The pond is typical for this forest, or for most of the mixed forests of the Norwegian lowlands. Hemmed in on the opposite side by thick coniferous forest.

On my side, the landscape is more open. A blend of long, slender pines and birches. Moors and marshes. Here and there, a bright hillcrest.

The pond is surrounded by marshes and floating peat bogs. Cotton grass grows here in the summer and fall, and the occasional cloudberry. Bilberry grows a bit farther in, where the soil is more solid, and waterlilies circle in the small inlets. But not right now. Now there is nothing.

The large boulder is rounded on the bottom and flat on top. It is cold, having cooled gradually throughout the fall. And it is very big. Perhaps five feet across, it must weigh half a ton, maybe more. How did it get here? It seems ill-placed in the flat landscape. There are no large mountains nearby, no natural source for such a rock. It must have landed here during the ice age. I don't know, of course, but that is my best guess. If there's one thing I have learned this year, it's how liberating it is to refer to the ice age whenever you need an explanation for strange natural formations.

I run my eyes over the campsite one last time. I will return again in the summer and several times in the following years, but not in the same way. I should probably feel a sense of sadness now, but I don't. I am wet and cold and thus not receptive to those kinds of emotions at the moment, and so I make it easy, tip my cap, turn, and start on the long trek back home.

As I walk, I think about Aristotle. I already suspected when I started writing this book that I would at some point drag the Greek philosopher into it. I'm happy I was able to hold off until December. Because, in fact, I've given a lot of thought to Aristotle all throughout the year. A surprising amount, actually. Aristotle was as much a naturalist as he was a philosopher. High and low at the same time, he was interested in everything around him, driven by a ceaseless curiosity about how the universe, of which he was a part, was configured. How it functions on every level, from the most concrete physical laws to the most advanced intellectual abstractions.

Aristotle used the term *telos* to describe the idea that all living things have an inherent purpose, a goal toward which they strive, and this goal is the thing's own realization. In the end, we all will die. I will die, the beaver I saw in June will die. But before we do, we will, according to Aristotle, struggle to realize our selves, to fulfill that which is our purpose on this earth, the reason we came into being. The beaver and I, two insignificant representatives of our own kinds, uninteresting in the greater context. But we are here, existing in precisely this moment, and we must do something with ourselves. The beaver builds and gnaws. When I observed it in the summer, it seemed to be obsessed with its compulsion to work. Almost manic, it could not rest, its inner nature told it there were more trees to fell—they were everywhere—and its dam could always be improved. Wasn't that a little breach down there at the surface? Wouldn't it be better to make the whole thing a little bit taller, a little bit wider? The beaver was driven by voices like that; it was its nature speaking to it, its *telos*, saying keep swimming, beaver, gnaw, chew, pull, push, drag. Save sleep for the winter months.

As I walk, the dawn light begins to brighten. The time is well past nine o'clock. On this final day in the woods, I have experienced seven hours of light and seventeen hours of darkness. I pass my lunch spot, where the river joins the lake, and continue past several small landmarks I recognize and feel are somehow partly mine. I arrive at the river that flows from the lake down in the valley. The river is always flowing; it is one of the few natural components that does not follow a daily cycle; it never stops moving. The water also has its *telos*: it runs toward a point that is lower than where it currently is. The goal is equilibrium, and as I walk I consider that maybe this is the overarching goal of nature, to reach a state of absolute harmony. Air that flows, rain that falls, steam that rises, ice that forms, and snow that melts. Everything is in motion all the time, and all of it strives toward a balance that only rarely occurs and can never last.

I have thought of this micro-expedition as a practice in line with the Aboriginal Australians' rite of passage called walkabout. I have not had any intended aim, nothing other than the desire to walk around in the woods at my leisure and with few, or no, tasks. This is what I've done, and what I will continue to do. If anyone ever asks me whether or not I'd recommend such a venture to others, I will respond with an unconditional yes. These twelve nights have affirmed my theory that very little is required to feel as if you are the main character in a fairy tale. It is as simple as that. There are forests everywhere. All that's required is to venture into them.

In spite of the lack of aim for my expedition, I feel the final leg should have a conclusion of sorts. I feel an expectation to come up with some type of clever insight as I walk the last few yards down to the car. Some secret experience that I can reveal to this book's readers from which they might benefit, a small pearl of wisdom hidden to all except those who wander alone in the woods.

If there is any such wisdom to be had, it would have to be something like this:

Many of us live in a day and an age and in parts of the world where, now more than ever before, we are told that we are worthy, that we mean something, that we are special. The individual is elevated in every context: we are all supposed to realize our true selves, preferably to the sound of everyone else's applause.

In such a world, it is easy to lose perspective entirely, and I believe that the woods, for my part, or the mountains, or the ocean, or whatever kind of nature we have at our doorstep, beckons to us because it represents a point outside of this individual-centric culture that bombards us on every side. We need this nature, and it is our obligation to take care of it.

Our culture insists that each of us is unique. Nature tells us the opposite, and thus offers a necessary corrective. You are not so big after all. Everything does *not* depend on you. We were here before you and we will be here after you, so stop making such a big deal out of it all.

There is a measure of comfort in the thought, and there is also meaning. So this is the only thing I take home with me from this micro-expedition, this year in the woods. It is a wise saying that I've either picked up along the way or else come up with completely on my own. I don't remember which, and it doesn't matter much: sometimes you have to be big enough to realize how very small you are.

# APPENDIX

## AN OFFICE WORKER'S
## WILDERNESS TIPS

N ENTIRE LITERARY genre exists on the topic of a life of solitude in the woods. This is a genre that frequently embellishes the truth and in which authors often neglect to mention their own shortcomings. Another related genre explains how to get by in the wild: books brimming with practical advice and instructions on how to solve various challenges, what to wear, what to eat, what equipment to bring along, and a whole lot of other more or less useful things. Books in this genre are also supposedly written by people with an overwhelming knowledge of nature and how best to handle oneself in it. There's not a single thing these folks haven't experienced or for which they haven't devised some nifty solution. These are the books of our times, easy to market and easy to write. I've read a lot of these kinds of books, not only in preparation for my micro-expedition but also, from the comfort of my bed, as pure entertainment. While Trude has invested her time in reading award-winning novels or nonfiction about something important, I've read chapters with titles like "How to Build a Split-Log Fire" or "Three Tips for Avoiding Condensation in the Tent."

After twelve nights in the woods, I myself feel a measure of pressure to add my own pebble to this cairn of outdoor tips. Therefore, as a conclusion of sorts, I will attempt to give some down-to-earth, sensible advice to any reader who feels inspired to spend a night in the woods, alone or with others, after having read this book. These tips are based on my own experiences from this year in the woods, and I have listed them in no particular order whatsoever, the way it often is with knowledge gathered through experience.

As one overarching tip, I would like to say this: life in the woods is fundamentally practical. You learn by doing, and after only a single night out you will have gained a surprising amount of new knowledge. Thus, be careful not to assume that all your advance preparation will be sufficient or that all of the gear you buy will be the only gear you'll need. Be prepared for the fact that you may constantly have to make adjustments—this is a valuable part of the experience.

## TENT, SLEEPING BAG, SLEEPING PAD, AND BACKPACK

These are the four basic pieces of outdoor equipment, and there are so many options that it requires an expedition just to get a handle on all of them. When it comes to a tent, it's impossible to know whether the tent will be right for your needs until you've actually tried it out. Thus, the best thing you can do is go to the kind of store that has floor models already set up so you can crouch down, crawl inside, and get a feeling for what each tent is like.

When it comes to sleeping bags, I recommend that you buy a four-season down bag that has a temperature rating of about 15 degrees Fahrenheit. Down is compressible and light, so the sleeping bag won't take up that much space in your backpack. It can be cold at some latitudes even in July, so my experience is that so-called "summer" sleeping bags are best for interrail trips in Southern Europe, camping trips in the American Southwest, or sleeping inside of a cabin or some-one's house. You can use a four-season bag year-round, and only a very few people sleep outside below fifteen degrees.

Modern sleeping pads are inflatable and very thin and take up hardly any space when compressed. Mine constantly got punctured, and I always found it uncomfortable to lie on because it was slippery and wobbly and made a lot of noise whenever I moved. I ended up going back to a sleeping pad made of closed-cell foam that I hooked onto the back of my backpack. It is indestructible and cost almost nothing.

My most valuable piece of advice about backpacks is as follows: don't buy one that is too big. The larger your pack, the more stuff you are automatically going to fill it with. Trudging around with a backpack that is too heavy greatly diminishes enjoyment of the outdoor experience. I am five feet, eleven inches tall and I carry an 80-liter backpack. I think this is too big. I should have bought one that is only 60 liters, or 70 max. That would have forced me to pack more rationally.

## CLOTHING

I have always used a wool turtleneck sweater on my backpacking trips to the woods, and so it is not without some difficulty that I have to admit the superiority of fleece and PrimaLoft materials. Fleece is very warm and dries easily. PrimaLoft is very warm, dries easily, and in addition is extremely compressible. Still, I've always brought along a wool sweater on my nights in the woods, primarily for sentimental reasons. It's up to you, but you should be aware that a thick wool sweater can quickly fill up half a backpack. Closest to your feet, however, you should definitely opt for wool socks. Every good Norwegian knows this.

A shell rain jacket and pair of rain pants are essential, though I have often just worn a regular pair of hiking pants made of cotton or a water-resistant softshell material—and something similar on my upper body. When the weather is nice, these fabrics are much easier to move about in. They breathe better—and when it rains, you are going to have to put on something waterproof anyway. My Gore-Tex jacket leaked like a sieve, but there are undoubtedly other better options.

I always bring rain pants and a rain jacket with me; that is, a top and bottom that *isn't* breathable and is therefore totally waterproof. If it's coming down hard and you aren't moving, this is the only solution. Good boots are essential, but of course you already knew that. In my experience, the modern Gore-Tex boots far exceed the old ones made of leather.

## COOKING GEAR

No one who ventures out for a night in the woods needs to bring along a fully stocked kitchen with a sauté pan, coffee-pot, and three or four pots and pans of various sizes. Save yourself the space and weight. I brought along a single pot that was narrow with high sides and had a small lid—it was fast and easy to boil water in. On a few of my nights outside, I brought a sauté pan but I quickly realized I didn't need it. You can fry anything in the bottom of your regular pot or cook it on a stick over an open fire. You can also use the pot for boiling water for coffee, and if your coffee carries a hint of bacon, not to worry: you'll get used to it. I used an ordinary gas burner that is small and light in weight, and a gas canister.

If you are backpacking with other people you should probably consider bringing a plate to keep up the appearance that you are civilized, but if you're on your own you can just eat straight out of the pot. You'll need a fork, a spoon, and a good camping cup. When you are backpacking in the winter, it's best to choose a thermos cup so your coffee doesn't surprise you by turning cold immediately. A little tin of salt and pepper (which you can mix beforehand) and a tin of butter are essential. And last but not least: a water bottle made of some indestructible material that is easy to access while you are walking.

## OTHER GEAR AND TOOLS

A knife is the most important wilderness tool. I would recommend an ordinary knife that is good for whittling. The
handle should feel good in your hand and the blade should
not be too long. It's easy to be tempted to buy a knife that's
too big—it makes you feel a lot tougher—however, the average hiker has no need for a long knife blade. I bought a knife
that could also supposedly function as an axe. That's what
the advertisement claimed. It was a fiasco: the knife was bad
at whittling and bad at chopping, and in my zeal to get two
things for one, I ended up with a useless object.

If you live in a place like Norway, you'll want to bring
along a little mosquito net in the summer that you can wrap
around your head. Midges and gnats can be unbearable and
there's no escaping them. These head nets pack down to the
size of a matchbox and hardly cost anything. You can get
them in a variety of colors, and I myself have tried them out
in green, black, and white. I have to say I like the green one
best of all because it's the easiest to see through.

Don't rely on your smartphone when you are out in the
woods. Remember, you could lose coverage at any moment.
I have sometimes used the GPS on my phone, but it isn't
necessary. I always bring along a map inside a waterproof
plastic sleeve on my hikes, not only in case I get lost but also
because I like to study the map and look for new paths and
unfamiliar places. Studying the map is a pleasant activity
when you are inside the tent, before nodding off to sleep in
the evening and after waking up in the morning.

## PACKING

Nothing is more important than staying warm. Prioritize your clothing, sleeping bag, and sleeping pad over everything else, but also be sure not to take too much. When it comes to clothing, the principle is to bring two of every item that you wear closest to your skin and to make sure they are quick-drying. If one piece of clothing gets wet, you can put on the other one and dry out the first. Always be aware that you have a much higher likelihood of packing too much than too little. The larger your backpack, the more you are going to put into it.

## IMPORTANT ROUTINES

Always bring your water bottle with you into the tent at night. In the winter, some people opt to bring in a bottle to pee in as well. This is not only for the sake of comfort, but also because you risk losing a lot of heat by leaving your sleeping bag in the middle of the night, venturing outside, and getting cold—only to return to your sleeping bag and have to warm it up all over again.

You should establish routines about where and how to store your matches or lighters. Always bring at least two, and put one of them in an easy-to-find location, sealed off in your backpack where you don't store a lot of other items. I always put one in the little pocket inside the lid of my backpack. That's where I also store my first-aid kit, car keys, wallet, and cell phone. Go ahead and pack some fire starter as well, to make it easy to ignite your campfire if it's wet out. For more experienced hikers, or for those who don't want to bring too many things, you might want to pack a few pieces of birchbark or something similar.

## DAILY RHYTHMS AND SEASONS

I have given a lot of thought to this topic throughout my year in the woods. Where bedtime is concerned, I would recommend the following: in the winter, don't go to sleep too early. It might feel cozy, but if you decide to do it, you should expect to wake up very early in the morning. In the spring, I recommend going to bed early and getting up early. Both the evening and the morning are nice in the spring, but if I had to choose one or the other, it would have to be the morning. From April onward, you shouldn't get up any later than five a.m. In the summer, I recommend that you get up early and go to bed late. This might sound paradoxical. But if you get tired, you can snooze for a few hours during the day. In the fall, things once again tend toward darkness. Then the same rules apply as in winter.

## ARE THERE ANY OBJECTS FROM
## CIVILIZATION YOU SIMPLY CAN'T DO WITHOUT?

I always bring something to read. It gets dark early in the winter. You are most likely going to be spending a lot of time inside your tent. A headlamp is, of course, essential for being able to see the book's contents. It is also necessary if you want to do anything else outside in the wintertime. Remember to pack extra batteries, enclosed in a dry, water-proof case of sorts and stored in an easily accessible location, such as with the first-aid gear and your extra matches.

Finally, wherever you go, in Norway or anywhere else in the woods at any time of year: remember to bring your beanie.

# NOTES

The definition of nature on page 1 is from *Store Norske Leksikon (The Great Norwegian Encyclopedia)*. English translation by Becky L. Crook © 2021. Used by permission of Andreas Tjernshaugen, *Store Norske Leksikon*, snl.no.

The quote on page 28 is from Kathleen Jamie's *Sightlines*, The Experiment, 2013. Used by permission of the author and The Experiment.

The excerpt on page 50 is from Werner Herzog's film *Grizzly Man*, Discovery Docs and Lions Gate Films, 2005, 103 minutes. Used by permission of Werner Herzog.

The excerpt from Karl Ove Knausgård on page 72 is from *Min kamp 1*, Forlaget Oktober, 2009. This English excerpt first appeared in Archipelago Books's *My Struggle: Book One*, by Karl Ove Knausgård, translated from the Norwegian by Don Bartlett © 2012. Used by permission of the publishers and translator Don Bartlett.

# SOURCES

WHILE WORKING ON this book, I thought about a lot of the books that made a big impression on my younger self. I still have some of them on my bookshelf, but most of them are now only in my memory. Some I've re-read and others I've merely tried to recall. I can't name all of them here, but I will list some of the books I've come to read in later years which have been important for my work on *A Year in the Woods*. I don't have any illusions that this bibliography is representative for all the literature that is available about nature and a life outdoors. Nor have I tried to be very systematic in compiling my list—the books here have to do with my own preferences. My wish has not been to provide a treatise on nature, but rather a subjective telling in which I reflect on my own experiences. Nevertheless, these books—and many others that I don't have the space to name here—have contributed to widening my perspectives about nature and the human relationship to it as well as to other related topics that I have written about. They are listed here in alphabetical order as a little bonus for anyone who feels inspired to dig deeper in the literary genre on nature.

Many of these books are only available in Norwegian, though this list might still be interesting to readers and publishers interested in the topics here.

Ambjørnsen, Ingvar. *Natten drømmer om dagen* (*The Night Dreams of the Day*). Cappelen Damm, 2012.

Bryson, Bill. *A Walk in the Woods*. Black Swan, 1998.

Cappelen, Peder W. *Alene med vidda* (*Alone on the Plateau*). Gyldendal Norsk Forlag, 1964.

Cappelen, Peder W. *Vidda på ny* (*The Plateau Again*). Gyldendal Norsk Forlag, 1974.

Chatwin, Bruce. *The Songlines*. Vintage Books, 1998.

Clausen, Kristoffer og Gunnar Omsted. *En vill mann. 365 dager som jeger, fisker og sanker* (*A Wild Man: 365 Days as Hunter, Fisher, and Gatherer*). Cappelen Damm, 2010.

Dahl, Johannes. *Nordmarka. Eventyr og Eldorado* (*The Nordmarka Forest: Adventure and Eldorado*). Johan Grundt Tanum, 1942.

Dahlby, Frithiof. *Grei deg selv. Små tips for speidere og andre friluftsfolk* (*Take Care of Yourself: Small Tips for Scouts and Other Outdoor Folks*). Gimnes Forlag, 1949.

*Den Norske Turistforening:* Østlandske skogsområder.
   *Fjell og Vidde* 7, 1994.

*Den Norske Turistforenings Aarbok for 1868.* Det Steenske
   Bogtrykkeri, 1868.

Freud, Sigmund. *Unbehaget i kulturen (Civilization and
   Its Discontents).* J. W. Cappelens Forlag, 1992.

Frislid, Ragnar. *På tur i skog og fjell. Håndbok for friluftsfolk
   (Hiking in Forests and Mountains: A Guidebook for Outdoor
   Enthusiasts).* J. W. Cappelens Forlag, 1967.

Gabrielsen, Bjørn. *Veien ut. En mann. En skog. Ett år. Ingen
   plan (The Way Out: A Man. A Forest. No Plan.).* Kagge, 2006.

Gopnik, Adam. *Winter: Five Windows on the Season.*
   Quercus, 2011.

Grieve, Guy. *Call of the Wild: My Escape to Alaska.* Hodder, 2007.

Herzog, Werner. *Grizzly Man.* Discovery Channel Inc., 2005.

Hessen, Dag O. *Natur: hva skal vi med den? (Nature: What
   Should We Do with It?).* Gyldendal, 2008.

Holtvedt, Reidar. *Fra Nordmarka og Krokskogen (From the
   Nordmarka and Krokskogen).* Aschehoug, 1972.

Humphreys, Alastair. *Microadventures: Local Discoveries for Great Escapes*. William Collins, 2014.

Ingstad, Helge. *Pelsjegerliv: Blant Nord-Canadas indianere* (The *Fur Trapper's Life: Among Northern Canada's Indigenous Peoples*). Gyldendal, 2001.

Jamie, Kathleen. *Findings*. Sort Of Books, 2005.

Jamie, Kathleen. *Sightlines*. Sort Of Books, 2012.

Keith, Sam, and Richard Proenneke. *One Man's Wilderness: An Alaskan Odyssey*. Graphic Arts Center Publishing, 2006.

Kent, Rockwell. *Wilderness: A Journal of Quiet Adventure in Alaska*. G. P. Putnam's Sons, 1920.

Krakauer, Jon. *Into the Wild*. Pan Books, 2007.

Lees, J. A., and W. J. Clutterbuck. *Three in Norway by Two of Them*. Longmans, Green & Co., London, 1888.

Maclean, Norman. *A River Runs through It and Other Stories*. The University of Chicago Press, 2001.

Moland, Tallak. *Historien om Nordmarka gjennom de siste 200 år* (The *History of the Nordmarka through the Last 200 Years*). Christiania Forlag, 2006.

Monsen, Lars. *101 Villmarkstips (101 Wilderness Tips)*.
Larsforlaget, 2011.

Næss, Arne. *Ecology, Community, and Lifestyle*. Translated
and edited by David Rothenberg. Cambridge University Press, 1989.

Næss, Jan Chr., and Bård Løken. *Inn i naturen (Into Nature)*.
N. W. Damm & Søn, 2007.

Nansen, Fridtjof. *Eventyrlyst*. Edited by Erling Kagge.
Cappelens Forlag AS, 1995.

Øverås, Tor Eystein. *I dette landskap. Artikler og essays*.
*(In This Landscape: Articles and Essays)*. Gyldendal, 2012.

Pettersen, Marius Nergård. *Oslos nære villmark (Oslo's
Nearby Wilderness)*. Cappelen Damm, 2013.

Proenneke, Richard. *Alone in the Wilderness*. Bob Swerer
Productions, 2003 and 2011.

Snyder, Gary. *The Practice of the Wild*. Counterpoint
Berkeley, 1990.

Solnit, Rebecca. *A Field Guide to Getting Lost*. Canongate, 2006.

Solnit, Rebecca. *Wanderlust: A History of Walking*. Penguin Books, 2001.

Sørensen, Øystein. *Kampen om Norges sjel 1770–1905. Norsk idéhistorie bind III (The Fight for Norway's Soul, 1770–1905: Norwegian History of Ideas, volume III)*. Aschehoug, 2001.

Stafford, Ed. *Walking the Amazon. 860 Days. The Impossible Task. The Incredible Journey*. Virgin Books, 2011.

Szymborska, Wisława. "Livet er den eneste måten" ("Life is the Only Way," a poem from 2002–2012). Translated into Norwegian by Christian Kjelstrup. Tiden, 2013.

Thoreau, Henry David. *Walden—Or Life in the Woods*. Random House, 1992.

Trømborg, Dagfinn. *Geologi og landformer i Norge (Geology and Land Formations in Norway)*. Tun Forlag, 2006.

Wiese, Jan. *Jeg skal til Katnosa i kveld (I'm Off to Katnosa Tonight)*. J. W. Cappelens Forlag, 1979.

Zappfe, Peter Wessel. *Barske glæder. Og andre temaer fra et liv under åpen himmel (Rough Joys, and Other Themes from a Life Lived under the Open Sky)*. Cappelen Damm, 2012.

# GRATITUDE

T O THE FOLKS at *Harvest* magazine, Kjetil, Simen, and Anders, for having the same idea as me and doing something about it. To my Norwegian editor, Sverre, who understood what I wanted to write about and why, and who let me do exactly that. To Tarje, for priceless conversations underway. To Jørn and Geir, who helped me to believe that the things I was writing might also be meaningful for others. And to Trude and Helena and August, who allowed me to go to the woods over the course of the entire year, and who listened patiently to my long stories every time I came back.